A CHARTWELL-BRATT STUDE[

CW00741955

An Introduction to the
Unix Operating System
2nd Edition

Craig Duffy

Department of Computer Studies and Mathematics
Bristol Polytechnic

 Chartwell-Bratt

 Studentlitteratur

To MRF

British Library Cataloguing-in-Publication Data
A catalogue record for this book is available from the British Library.

© Craig Duffy and Chartwell-Bratt 1991.

Chartwell-Bratt (Publishing and Training) Ltd
ISBN 0-86238-271-8

Printed in Sweden
Studentlitteratur, Lund
ISBN 91-44-27612-5

Printing   1 2 3 4 5 6 7 8 9 10 | 1996 95 94 93 92 91

Table of Contents

Preface

This short book is the result of both practical experience using various UNIX systems, and of study into UNIX and operating systems in general. Many people will find that there are some curious omissions. For example shell script programming receives no coverage and the **chgrp** command is not described. Some of these omissions are because they, in the case of shell script programming, merit more coverage than I felt I could give in the present book. Shell script programming itself would merit an entire book dedicated to it. Other things have been left out simply because I do not use them or have not found them particularly useful. This is not to say they are of no use, but just that I have, so far, had no use for them.

This book was written using a Gould PN6000 computer, with, believe it or not, some help from a LSI 11–23 running Edition 7 UNIX. The Gould runs a combination of ATT system V version 2 and Berkeley version 3.2. So most of the book will be applicable to most UNIX machines. The document was produced using the Gould and an Apple Macintosh.

Although this book, and all the mistakes that sail in her, is the result of my labours, I must acknowledge some of the help I have received. The members of staff at Sheffield ITeC; Clinton Caine, Jean Cooper, Julia Dick, David Elliott, Wendy Miller, Debbie Prenz, and Ian Williams, plus all the students past and present. I should also like to particularly thank my colleague at Bristol Polytechnic, Rob Williams, for reading several drafts, and Kay Hunter from the Computing Centre. Finally I must thank Marta for putting up with this book for so long.

Preface to the Second Edition

I should like to thank Marta for being so supporting and Rob Williams for once again reading through the chapters. The diagrams are by Onnik Krikorian.

Foreword

The background to UNIX

The UNIX operating system was developed at Bell Laboratories in the United States of America. Bell Labs had initially been working on a joint project, with the Massachusetts Institute of Technology and General Electric, to develop the MULTICS operating system. MULTICS was specified as a multi-tasking time sharing computer operating system, and it was intended to give an on-line interactive computing facility, as opposed to the non-interactive batch systems that were common at that time (the mid 1960s). Bell Labs withdrew from the project before MULTICS was finally developed. Although MULTICS was finally released and is a working operating system which broke new ground in computer operating systems, it was such a large and unwieldy system that it never really became popular. So the programmers at Bell Labs found themselves without an operating system that suited them.

A small group of programmers got together and using a PDP-7 computer, began to design an operating system. Two Bell Labs employees, Ken Thompson and Dennis Ritchie did the major work developing this new system. In 1970 a member of the Bell Labs team, Brian Kernighan coined the name UNIX for the operating system. The first Edition of UNIX, there being a tradition that the releases of UNIX are known as editions after the publication of their manuals, was brought out in 1971. Further editions were released during the early seventies.

Concurrent with the development of UNIX, the programming language C was developed by Dennis Ritchie at Bell Labs. It initially grew out of the programming language BCPL, which is a low level language suited for developing operating systems. The language B was developed out of BCPL, and out of B developed C, no one has yet had the nerve to announce the successor language D. Despite being in its early stages C proved to be a popular language due to its power and terseness, and many UNIX utilities were, at least partly, written in C.

C has since gone on to become a success in its own right, and is now a very popular and widely used language. In 1973 UNIX was rewritten, being translated from its original PDP assembler to the new C language. This meant that UNIX was, potentially, a very portable operating system as it was no longer written in a machine specific language.

UNIX was initially used in Bells Labs for text formatting and document preparation, but its fame began to spread to the outside world. In 1975 Edition 6 was released and was made widely available. This meant that Colleges and Universities could, for the price of a tape, get a source code version of UNIX. All the college had to do was to mount the UNIX system onto their machine. By the time of the Seventh Edition (1979), to many UNIX in its purest form, Bell Labs management began to realise that UNIX was a very popular product, and the licensing agreement was made more restrictive to protect this product.

Why has UNIX become so popular?

There are many reasons for this. Firstly unlike the MULTICS project, and many other operating system projects of the time, UNIX is the product of a small group of professional computing specialists who had a series of practical aims to achieve. They worked with limited resources, apart from an over abundance of intellect and enthusiasm, and so produced an operating system that is reasonably comprehensible to programmers and users. UNIX in many ways is a very personalised system, unlike the impersonalised giants produced by the computing industry at that time.

The kernel of UNIX, the central core of the operating system, was kept small and reasonably simple. It does not attempt to offer hundreds of different commands or options, its tasks are limited to process management and file store maintenance. This means, for example, that when a user wishing to see the contents of a file in a particular directory, must run a separate program, as the kernel does not support such commands. This high level of factoring means that the kernel is good at what it does, and is uncluttered by others features. It also means that there can be great flexibility with the programs that make up UNIX. Rather than being a very robust, integrated, monolithic structure like VAX/VMS, UNIX is a very flexible set of well designed tools.

As UNIX is mainly written in the C programming language, apart from the benefits in making it easy for anyone who understands C to understand it, it is also very portable. This means that when using a UNIX system on one particular machine, it is relatively simple to transfer to a different machine that is running UNIX. Combining this with the relatively small size of the UNIX kernel and the ease of comprehension of UNIX as a whole, this means that porting (moving) it from one machine to another is not such a daunting task.

The high degree of factoring of the UNIX kernel also lead to another feature which has aided its success, in that the command line interpreters, known in UNIX speak as a shell, have been developed separately from the core of the operating system. This has produced some excellent user interfaces that are neither monstrously difficult to understand nor trivially simple to learn and exhaust. The quality of the shells and of the other UNIX utilities has ensured that UNIX will have a lasting effect in the computer market.

Finally it is worth mentioning that UNIX also had the advantage of good timing. It was developed just as the growth in the mini-computer market was taking off and has been sustained by the development of single processor 'super-micros' and networked work stations. Compared to the other alternatives around, the dinosaurs from the main frame market and the file handling utilities from the personal computer market, the success of UNIX becomes less surprising.

So what of the more recent history of UNIX?

There have been two major trends. Bells Labs combined many of the popular forms of UNIX into a newer version, called UNIX System III, which was later developed into the UNIX System V. At the same time a group at University of California at Berkeley developed their own version of UNIX, the latest being known as the Berkeley 4.3 Release. There have been other UNIX imitators around, some successful, some not. The majority of this book will be of relevance to both System V and Berkeley 4.n users.

The recent release of System V.4 has further developed UNIX as an industry standard. It implements such ideas as having a common object file format (COFF), which means that object files from different compilers can be linked, the application binary interface (ABI), which allows binaries to run on machines from different vendors running the same architecture processors, and the development of a standard graphical user interface (GUI) should mean that applications will have a similar look-and-feel. If the manufacturers who have thus far supported these moves continue to then UNIX should continue apace as a standard operating system.

Edward Gibbon, the historian of the Roman Empire, noted the tendency of success to have in its heart a fatal contradiction. Societies become enervated by the fruits of their success. Once powerful and virile nations become fat and weak with their gains and become prey to fanaticism and the looting of surrounding barbarians. Well UNIX has not quite reached this stage. It seems to be reaching its 'middle age' in reasonably good condition. Whilst it is showing a certain amount of paunch around the middle it is still capable of moving around at reasonable speeds. Whatever its future within the computing industry, it has certainly made its mark and will effect any other operating system design that may come along.

How to read this book

If you have managed thus far this advice is of necessity limited. The book can be read from cover to cover, and be used by the first time user as a guide to the UNIX system. It expects little previous knowledge of computers or computer operating systems, however access to a UNIX system would be a distinct advantage. A knowledge of a programming language, Pascal or C, for example, would also be advantageous, but not strictly necessary. Alternatively the book can be read in a random fashion, as few sections really require the knowledge learnt in the earlier sections. So hopefully the more advanced reader will find that there are things in this book for them. Realistically the only way to learn to use UNIX is by actually sitting in front of a terminal and trying out commands.

The best way to use this book is to experiment with the commands and examples I have given you. After you have read a bit, try it out. Don't worry about what commands you try as you can't hurt the machine, and it is best to find out which commands are dangerous when you have no files of any real importance. Above all enjoy using UNIX, that is what it's there for.

How To Login

The particular set up of your computer will regulate how you can login to it. On the system I use it is first necessary to select the machine I want from a port contender, and then login to UNIX after that choice has been made. In order to login to the system you will first have to make sure that you are an authorised user of the system. If you are unsure what that means then you had best go to the person or centre that provides your computing facilities and ask them if you can be a user.

Assuming that all that goes well, after turning on your terminal you should find yourself confronted with a prompt along the lines of:

Login:

At this prompt you should type in your user name:

Login: <u>lcs068</u> (or whatever)

Throughout this book I shall adopt the convention of all computer prompts and messages being in **bold** and for all of the user interactions that are typed in as a response being in **<u>bold underlined</u>**.

The computer may then prompt you for your password, and this may have been given to you along with your user number. To the prompt:

Password:

Type in your password, don't worry about anyone seeing it as it won't be echoed on the screen. If you don't have a password UNIX won't prompt you.

If all has gone well you should receive some general information and your command prompt:

%

This means that Unix is ready and waiting for commands. You can begin by typing:

%<u>news</u>

to see what is new on the system - everything will be new to you but don't worry about it. The news will probably go shooting by so press control s to hold up the display. This simply means holding down the key marked **CTRL** and pressing the **s** key at the same time, pressing control q will restart the display. If there is no news the prompt will simply be returned to you for further commands.

You may wish to alter your password from the one that you were given, or give yourself a password. Both of these things can be done with the **passwd** command. Type in:

%**passwd**

If you don't have a password then you will be prompted to type a new one in, and then prompted to retype it in case you made a mistake. Assuming it all went well, then this password will be the one you are prompted for when logging in until you decide to change it. If you already have a password, then you will be prompted for it before you can make a change to it. Users can only change their own passwords, although there is one user, known as super user or root, who effectively owns the whole system, who can change any password.

If your system is a networked system using SUN's Networked File System (NFS) you may have to use the command **yppasswd**. This will work exactly like the **passwd** command above, although it may take longer for your password to register on other machines in your network. To find out which password command to use ask your local system manager.

UNIX normally distinguishes between upper case and lower case characters. All system commands are in lower case. If when you logged onto the system your terminal had the shift/alpha lock key depressed, then UNIX will assume that your terminal can only work with capital letters, and it will ignore the distinction between upper and lower case. If this happens you can either, type in:

%**stty -lcase**

This will let your terminal have lower and upper case, don't worry how it does it just for the moment. Alternatively you can logoff the system and login in lower case (with alpha/shift lock turned off).

Logging off

You can logoff the system in two ways. One is to press ^d (control d). It will look a bit as if UNIX is waiting for input, but don't worry you will have been logged off. To prove it press return a few times and the login prompt will reappear. Alternatively you can type:

%**logout**

This will have the same effect as **^d**. If after asking to logout, either by **^d** or **logout**, UNIX replies:

There are stopped jobs

this means that some time whilst executing a command you pressed **^z** or **^y** (control z or control y). This had the effect of putting the current job into the background to be finished off at some later date, and UNIX is telling you that you have not finished this job. To override this check give the logout command twice in succession. For more information on what **^z** and **^y** do see the section on history and environment .

learn

On the UNIX system there is a suite of programs that give beginners a tutorial introduction to UNIX. To run these programs type in:

%**learn**

Learn will then provide a series of menus, and can adequately guide the novice.

The UNIX Operating System

Introduction

The UNIX operating system is made up of three parts; the kernel, the shell and the utilities.

1) The kernel, normally the file/unix. This is the UNIX operating system properly speaking. The kernel contains all the system primitives, it deals with all the hardware devices (terminals, printers, etc) and it does all I/O work.

2) The Shell. This is normally the file /bin/csh (pronounced 'see shell') or /bin/sh (the Bourne shell). The shell is the command line interpreter. It parses command lines, does wild card, variable and history substitutions. The shells have quite advanced command structures, and are programmable.

3) The utilities, known variously as the tools or filters. They are a series of programs, available as standard on UNIX systems. They generally do some form of manipulation on text files.

The diagram, figure one, is not meant to be representative of any hierarchal relationship between the shell and utilities.

To understand the difference between the different parts of UNIX, let us look at the differing ways we come to see UNIX. When a computer is started up, running UNIX, after it has gone through a sequence known as booting up, a program, normally the file called /**unix**, is executed. This program known as the kernel, will remain resident in memory through out the period that UNIX is running on the machine.

The kernel does all of the low level work of the operating system. It is a very large program that maintains all the running processes on the system, manages the file system, has responsibility for allocating

THE 3 PARTS OF UNIX

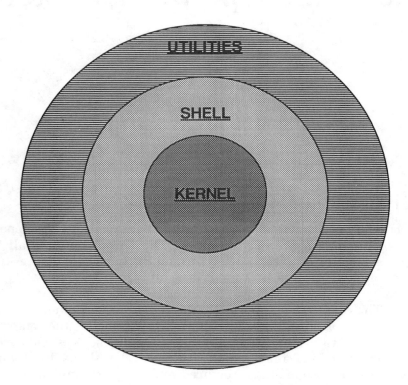

Figure 1. The kernel, shell and utilities

memory and disk space. The kernel is written in C and is a series of functions to do particular tasks. These different functions can be called, like other C functions, from other programs running on the UNIX system. These calls are known as system calls. In order for any process to run, to create files, access the disk, etc, it must go through the kernel. The kernel is one of the few pieces of code that is non-optional.

However as it is not feasible to write programs that deal with the machine at such a low level, an interface between the kernel and the user is provided. This is known in UNIX as a shell. Being a command line interpreter, most of its features are to help users to interact with the machine more effectively. It is possible to have a wide variety of shells on the UNIX system, and indeed it is possible to switch from one to the other. The shell has its own built-in commands, its own primitives or 'system calls', but its main feature is to execute other programs.

The programs the shell executes are generally known as the utilities. There is no intrinsic difference between a program written by any user on a UNIX system and the utilities that come with the operating system. They are all dealt with in the same way by the shell and kernel. UNIX comes with a wide variety of useful utility programs. The ones which are of the most interest to us are the programs called filters, that take some stream of text input and produce a stream of text output. There are also utilities for manipulating files, for aiding writers, programming languages and doing software development.

So what happens when a user types in a command. Take for example this command line:

%**cat** *

The prompt % is provided by the command line interpreter. The kernel is not suited for interactive programming and has no interactive features. The command **cat** is a UNIX utility, that can be used to output the contents of specified files to the terminal screen. It is an ordinary, albeit useful, program that is written in C. The * is a special character, called a wild card, used by the shell, and it substitutes into all the file names in the current directory. So the line is asking UNIX to type out the contents of all the files in the current directory to the terminal screen. The command, **cat**, does not need to know anything about the wild card. In fact as far as **cat** is concerned it has simply been called with the list of the directory's files as its argument.

The involvement of the kernel in this activity is hidden. However in order to execute the line, or to see any information, the kernel must be invoked. In order to actually execute the **cat** command, the kernel must be asked to load it into memory and start it running. When the command wishes to look at contents of a file, the kernel must be invoked to locate the file, check that the program can do the things it wishes, and then supply the data. Nothing can be done without the involvement of the kernel. Even when attaching to a remote system the local kernel must be accessed and although it only acts as a conduit for the remote machine the kernel must filter all of the data passed.

3

Whenever someone refers to UNIX they will be talking about one, or a combination of kernel, shell or utilities. Which one it is will depend upon what kind of work is being done. A systems programmer will see the kernel as UNIX, whereas the average user will know the utilities very well and have little knowledge of the kernel. Most users will come to regard their favourite utilities as the essence of UNIX.

The File System

Everything on UNIX is a file. UNIX imposes no structure upon files. It treats them as a sequential series of bytes. A file will contain whatever you put into it, there are no hidden extras. It is common for many UNIX utilities to treat files as a series of ASCII characters[1] separated by carriage returns. However it is up to the programmer to enforce such standards. Hardware devices such as printers, discs, terminals etc are all treated in a standard way as files. There is no real difference between writing to an ASCII text file and writing to the printer – UNIX treats both of them as a simple sequence of bytes. It is easy to write programs on UNIX without worrying about the source or the destination of I/O.

There are 5 different types of files:

1) Ordinary files. These are the ones that contain data. They are created by users using editors, running compilers etc.

2) Directory files. These are files with pointers to other files. Access to read, write and remove directories is restricted to certain commands.

3) Device files. These are the hardware devices on the system. They are of two kinds – character or block device files. This is dependent on how they deal with data – ie. a terminal is a character device and a tape streamer is a block device.

4) Sockets. These are network nodes and are used for network access.

5) Pipes. Pipes are special files that are used to connect input and output between two processes.

---

[1]ASCII stands for American Standard Code for Information Interchange. It is the most widely used numeric code for representing characters in computers.

The Directory Structure

All the files are grouped together in the directory structure. The UNIX directory structure is an inverted tree hierarchy (see figure two). The top of the hierarchy is traditionally called "root". A directory may contain any number of files and subdirectories, which may be nested to any depth.

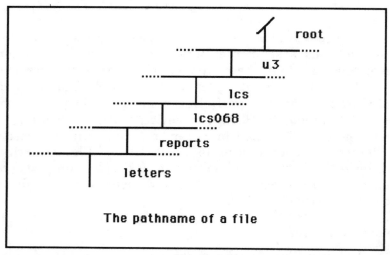

The pathname of a file

Figure 2

Path-names

To describe a file's location in the directory structure you have to give its path-name. That means writing out the name of each directory you pass through, separated by a slash character '/', in order to get to a file. To describe where the file **letters** is you would have to give the path;

/u3/lcs/lcs068/reports/letters

The leading slash means that the path-name starts at root's directory (root's directory is known as /). This is known as an **absolute path-name,** as it will describe the same path regardless of where the user is in the hierarchy.

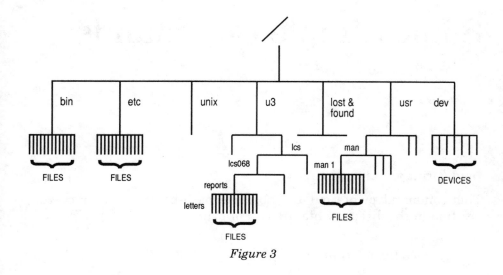

Figure 3

Files can also be described by **relative path-names**. This means describing them from a particular location in the directory hierarchy. If user lcc999 was in the directory /u3/lcs and wanted to refer to the file **letters**, she would type:

lcs068/reports/letters

Relative path-names do not have leading slash characters, and are dependent upon the current position of the user issuing them. If the path-name is mistyped or incorrect, UNIX will give a warning message and abort the command.

Some Simple Commands

pwd (**p**rint **w**orking **d**irectory)

This command prints out the absolute path-name for your current position in the directory hierarchy. For example:

%**pwd**
/u3/lcs/lcs068/doc

cd (**c**hange **d**irectory)

cd changes your position in the directory hierarchy. **cd** accepts any legal path-name as a parameter and will, assuming you have all the right permissions, move you to it. ie

%**cd /usr/local/sup/bin**

There are some special notations used with **cd**; "." means the current directory. Therefore

%**cd .**

means stay where you are; ".." means the parent of the current directory, therefore

%**cd ..**

will take you one directory up the hierarchy. **Cd** typed without any parameters will return you to your "home" directory, namely the directory that you start in when you login. Home directories can also be referred to by the tilde ~ character.

%**cd ~**

has the same effect as **cd** . It can be used to specify paths starting at your home directory.

%**cd ~/pascal**

changes to a directory **pascal** in the user's home directory. **~username** will change you, permissions excepted, to the directory of a particular user:

%**cd ~lcc440**

will change you to the home directory of user lcc440. All of these path-names will be acceptable to any other UNIX command that requires a path-name.

who

Who reports who is logged onto the system at the time that **who** is executed. It is called by

%**who**

and reports:

lcs068	**tty09**	**Dec 18 13:01**
lcs050	**tty02**	**Dec 18 11:42**
root	**console**	**Dec 18 09:12**

The fields are, username, terminal line they are logged onto, and the time they logged on. If your system is a networked system then you may wish to know who is logged onto other machines. There is a version of **who** for getting information about remote users, called **rwho**. Due to performance constraints this is often not implemented. All is not lost however, the command **rusers** will give a simple list of users, machine-by-machine, for the network. Due to the way in which **rusers** works it does not know how many machines are on the network, so to terminate the command type **^C**.

%**rusers**

9

```
gould1          cshroot a_greath tmp50 tmp48 tmp49
la_louche       n_goodwi
zugzwang        c_duffy
beefheart       wroot
rigel           a_clymer
gould2          cshroot cj_watts cj_watts ir_johns
j_saini
sirius          s_ali
sol             c_duffy root c_duffy root j_saini
vega            a_clymer
^c
```

ls (**l**ist **s**chema)

ls reports the contents of directories. **ls** can be given a path-name of a directory to report, or with no parameters it reports on the current directory. To look at the contents of the directory **/usr/spool/lpd** type:

> %<u>**ls /usr/spool/lpd**</u>

cat (con**cat**enate)

As its name implies **cat** is for combining files. However it is commonly used to show the contents of a file on a terminal. If the file is larger than the screen (ie more than 25 lines), **cat**'s output will shoot past you. To stop this use **^s** (control s) to freeze the screen and **^q** (control q) to restart it. It is wise to know what type of file you are looking at, as if it is an executable file produced by a compiler, then it will be full of control codes that will freeze up your terminal. To look at the file **read.me**, type:

> %<u>**cat read.me**</u>

file

file reports, to the best of its knowledge, what the type of a specified file is. ie:

> %<u>**file dubious**</u>

will report what type of file **dubious** is. It can be one of the following – ASCII text, commands text, English text or a source program – all of which are printable – alternatively it could be data or an executable file both which are not printable.

Typing **file *** will report on all the files in your current directory. * is the match all wild card on UNIX. The wild card character **?** can be used to match single character occurrences. Therefore

%**file *.c**

would match all file with the suffix **.c** regardless of the characters before the full stop. Whereas

%**file ?ouse**

would only match files with names like house, louse, mouse, as only one character is being wild card matched. Ranges of characters can be specified with alternates or ranges in square brackets, ie

%**ls [a,A]***

will report on all files that start with either a or A. Whilst

%**ls [i-m]ouse**

will report on files that begin with a character in the range of **i to m** inclusive, and end with the characters ouse. In the previous example, louse and mouse would be matched, but not house. The ranges can be anywhere in the file name.

%**file *[S,s]**

reports on all files ending with either **s** or **S**.

wc (**w**ord **c**ount)

To find out how large a file is the utility **wc** can be used.

%**wc /etc/termcap**

will report:

2132 8051 96616 /etc/termcap

This means that the file **/etc/termcap** has 2132 lines, 8051 words and 96616 characters. **wc** can be made to restrict its output to only lines, words or characters using **-l**, **-w** or **-c** respectively. Its default is **-lwc** . It is worth noting that the majority of UNIX commands accept arguments in the form **-c** where **c** is a particular switch for the command. The command is called

> %**wc -l /etc/termcap**

to count the number of lines in the termcap file. Most UNIX utilities expect their arguments to come directly after the command name, if

> %**wc /etc/termcap -l**

was typed, **wc** would attempt, and fail, to open a file called **-l**. Multiple arguments are given

> %**wc -lc /etc/termcap**

date

Date prints out the current date and time. It is called

> %**date**

and will report:

> **Wed Dec 31 13:57:50 GMT 1986**

lpr (line printer),lprm (line printer remove),lpq (line printer query)

lpr is the line printer program. The command

> %**lpr filename(s)**

will enter the specified file(s) onto the line printer queue located **/usr/spool/lpd**. The jobs are then spooled to be printed by the line print daemon **lpd**. Some options can be given with **lpr**. The default number of copies per print out will be one, to change it use

> %**lpr -#3 apology**

This would result in three copies of the file **apology** being printed. It is possible to change the banner on the burst page of the print out. Typing

%**lpr -J 'Plato' apology**

would print **Plato** on the burst page. The **-J** option changes the file name on the banner, using **-C**, it is possible to change the system name on the burst page.

You may find that your system has different printers on it, some of higher quality than others. You can use **lpr** to send your output to a different printer. If there is a print queue called **h** you would send your jobs by

%**lpr -Ph apology**

Obviously the names and actual details of what printers you have will be very system dependent. You may wish to be notified when your print job has been completed. Using the **-m** option will get **lpr** to do this.

lprm removes jobs from the line print queue

%**lprm job_no**

will remove the specified job from the line printer queue. To find out what your line printer job numbers are, you can use **lpq** to report what jobs are in the queue and their job numbers. Typing

%**lprm -**

will remove all your current jobs from the printer queue. It is possible to query different printer queues by using the **-P** option. So

%**lpq -Ph**

will get **lpq** to query the queue named **h**.

Creating Files

The simplest way to create a file is to use **cat** and redirect its output to a specified file, ie :

%**cat > mine**

{ the > symbol means redirect into – this will be explained later on} This will allow you to type characters in, including carriage returns. Pressing **^d** will close the file for input.

*** Caution cat > will destroy an existing file ***

This method is fine for very creating small files, however it is extremely cumbersome for correcting errors. Generally files are created using editors.

vi (**Vi**sual Editor)

There are many editors on the UNIX system. The standard ones are **ed** and **ex** the line editors, a stream editor **sed** and a screen editor **vi**. I shall give a brief introduction to **vi** . To use **vi** type:

%**vi solitude**

If the file **solitude** does not exist, **vi** will create it, if it already exists **vi** will read it in to an edit buffer. This will throw up a window with text to edit or a series of '~' to represent empty lines – that is lines that don't exist yet. At the bottom of the screen the words **new file** or some information about an existing one will appear.

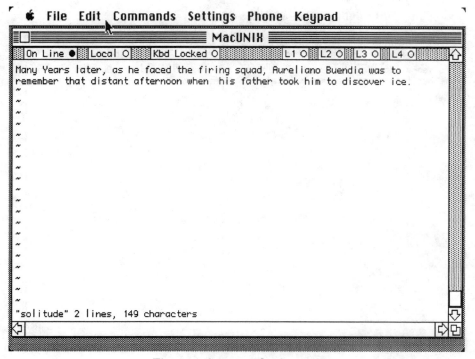

Figure 4. An example vi screen

There are two modes of operating in **vi** , command mode and insert mode. In command mode all key strokes are interpreted as commands and acted upon. In insert mode all key strokes are taken as text and entered into the document. **vi** works in command mode when it starts up.

To get into insert mode press **i**. Everything you type is inserted into the document before the character the cursor is on. In the above screen, for example, if the cursor were moved to the A of *Aureliano* and **i** was typed followed by the word *Colonel*, we would have:

15

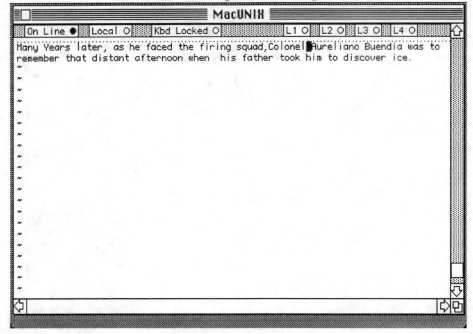

Figure 5

To get back to command mode press **esc** (escape). If at anytime you are unsure whether you are in command or insert mode, press **esc** twice. **Vi** will then beep at you indicating that you are in command mode.

In command mode you can move the cursor around using single key presses; **h** = back, **l**=forward,**j**=down,**k**=up – on most terminals you can use the cursor keys. To move a word at a time; **e**=word forward, **b**=word backward. To scroll the screen; **^u**=up,**^d**=down.

*** *caution make sure it is ^d (control d) * ***

It is possible to move the cursor to various locations on the current screen. **H** places it at the top left hand corner, **M** at the middle left hand side of the screen, and **L** places it at the bottom left hand corner of the screen. None of these requests will force the screen to scroll.

16

The cursor can be moved to a particular line with the **G** request, typing:

47G

will move the cursor to the beginning of the 47th line. Issuing **G** on its own moves it to the end of the file.

Inserting, Opening and Replacing

Insert mode can be reentered at any time. **a** appends after the character the cursor is on (**i** inserts before that character). **A** appends to the end of the current line. **I** inserts at the beginning of the current line. **o** opens a new line for input below the current line , **O** opens one above. **C** changes up to the end of the current line. **R** replaces from the current character, over typing the existing characters. All of these modes are exited by pressing **esc**.

With the cursor anywhere on the last line, if we typed **A** followed by some text:

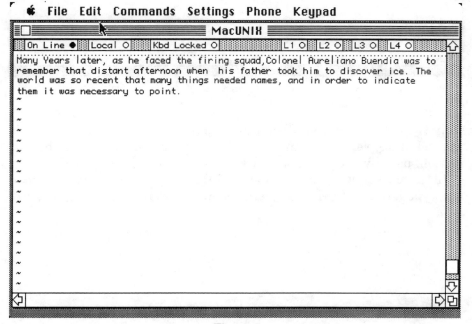

Figure 6

17

we would get the text beginning *the world* appended to the end of the line.

To replace the erroneous word *needed* with the correct word *lacked*, place the cursor on the *n* of *needed*, press **R**, type the correct words, followed by **esc**.

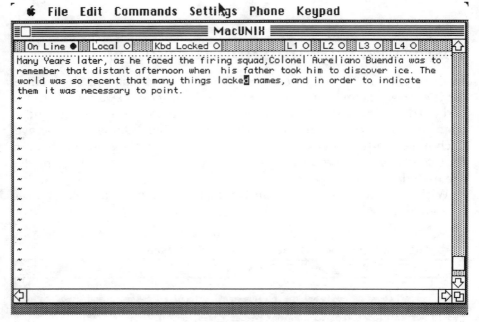

Figure 7

Only the 6 characters necessary are replaced. Obviously this example worked quite well as the incorrect word was the same size as the correction, usually one is not so lucky.

If the cursor was on the line beginning *"remember that"* , and **o** was typed, the text below would be open for input until **esc** is pressed.

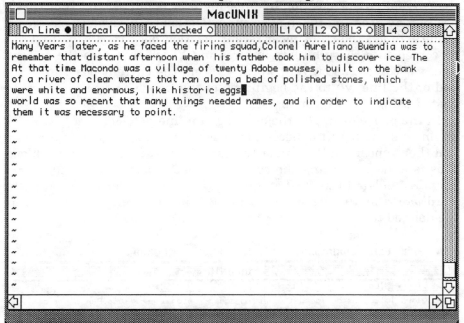

MacUNIX

| On Line ● | Local ○ | Kbd Locked ○ | L1 ○ | L2 ○ | L3 ○ | L4 ○ |

Many Years later, as he faced the firing squad,Colonel Aureliano Buendia was to
remember that distant afternoon when his father took him to discover ice. The
At that time Macondo was a village of twenty Adobe mouses, built on the bank
of a river of clear waters that ran along a bed of polished stones, which
were white and enormous, like historic eggs▮
world was so recent that many things needed names, and in order to indicate
them it was necessary to point.
~
~
~
~
~
~
~
~
~
~
~
~
~
~

Figure 8

Deletion and Pasting

To delete a single character, in command mode, press **x**. To delete a
word, from its first character, type **dw**, to delete a line type **dd**, to
delete to the end of the line from the current character type **d$**,to
delete from the current character to the beginning of the line type **d^**.
Most **vi** commands can be prefixed by a number which specifies the
amount of times you wish to repeat the action. Below are some examples:

4x	delete 4 characters
12dw	delete 12 words from the current word
36i*esc	insert 36 *s.
10j	move down the screen 10 lines
52dd	delete 52 lines (**vi** reports on any
	action that effects 6 lines or more)

19

Text that has been deleted can be reinserted into the document after the current cursor position by pressing **p** or before the current cursor position by pressing **P**. The last nine deletions are saved in a series of buffers, to get the third most recent deletion back type "**3p**. Text can be copied into these buffers by pressing **Y**, which copies the current line. **yw** copies the current word, **y$** from the current position to the end of the line, **y^** to the beginning of the line. The text can then be pasted using the **p/P** command.

In the above example, the opening of a line has left *"The"* stranded on line 4 stranded. It is necessary to cut it from the text into a buffer, and then reposition the cursor to paste the text into the correct place. This is done by moving the cursor to the *T* on the fourth line, pressing **d$** – delete to the end of the line. Then the cursor is moved to the word *world* at the beginning of line 10 and **P** is pressed to paste in the deleted text.

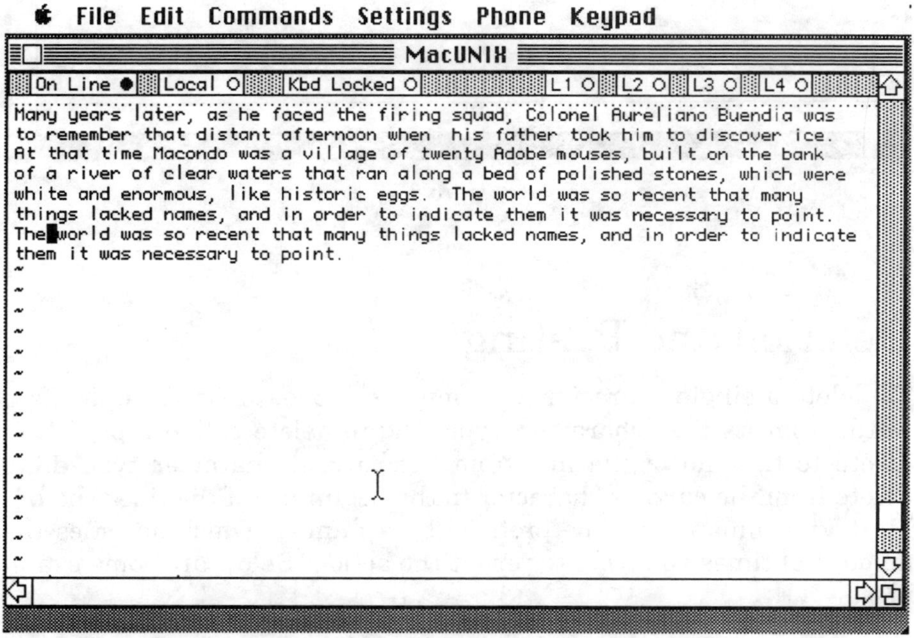

Figure 9

If you make a change by mistake, you can type **u** to undo the last change. To repeat the last command type '.'. So after the above instructions had we typed ' . . . ' we would end up with this:

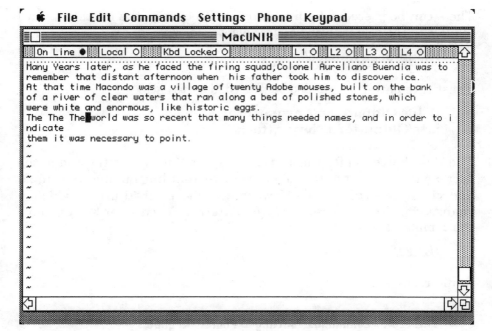

MacUNIX

On Line ● | Local O | Kbd Locked O | L1 O | L2 O | L3 O | L4 O

Many Years later, as he faced the firing squad, Colonel Aureliano Buendia was to
remember that distant afternoon when his father took him to discover ice.
At that time Macondo was a village of twenty Adobe mouses, built on the bank
of a river of clear waters that ran along a bed of polished stones, which
were white and enormous, like historic eggs.
The The The world was so recent that many things needed names, and in order to i
ndicate
them it was necessary to point.

Figure 10

Pressing **u** at this point could only get rid of one of the *The* 's. If we did not move off this line typing **U** would undo all changes made to it.

If at anytime you feel that the screen does not really reflect the state of the edit buffer, type **^r** to refresh the screen.

Searching and Substituting

Forward text searches can be done using **/pattern**. To search for the word *ate* type in **/ate**. However this will also find words such as *later*, *indicated* and so on. To search backwards from the current position use **?pattern**. Pressing **n** will force **vi** to search for the next occurrence of the pattern

To make text substitutions on the current line, first you need to go into line mode, by typing **:**. The general form is:

    :s/Oldpattern/Newpattern/

21

The **s** can be preceded by line numbers To change the mistaken word *mouses* to the correct word *houses* we would type:

:6s/mouses/houses/

Substitute patterns can also be preceded by ranges:

:1,10s/Oldpattern/Newpattern/
:.,$s/Oldpattern/Newpattern/

The '.' is shorthand for the current line, the **$** means to the end of the document. If you want to find out your current line number type in **:.=** and **vi** will report it to you. However the above substitutions will only change the first occurrence of Oldpattern in each line. For example the command:

:1,4s/a/i/

would result in:

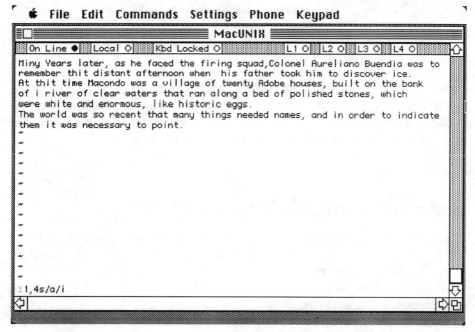

Figure 11

To force **vi** to substitute globally, ie not just the first occurrence on the line, you need the **g** suffix:

:1,$s/Oldpattern/Newpattern/g

Typing

:1,4s/a/i/g

would result in

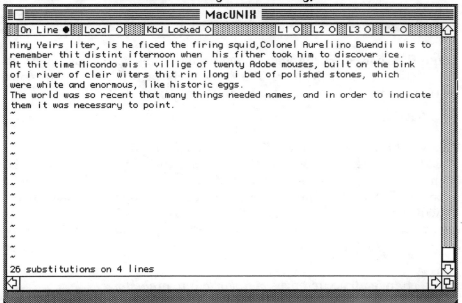

Figure 12

Using the **c** suffix makes **vi** prompt you with the pattern to be changed and a **^** prompt. The change will only occur by typing **y**. If the above command had been changed to:

:1,4s/a/i/gc

we would have been prompted:

Many years later, as he faced the firing
^

for each substitution. The effect of the substitution can be undone by typing the **u** command. This will only work if **u** is pressed before any other changes are made to the file. The last substitution can be repeated by typing **&**.

The substitution pattern can contain certain meta-characters to make the search pattern more specific. The **^** operator restricts the substitution to the beginning of the line. Typing

:1,25s/^House/Home/

will only change *House* to *Home* if it is at the beginning of the line. Typing

:1,$s/^At/at/

would therefore only change the beginning of line occurrence of **At** on line 3, in the example text. The **$** meta-character in an expression restricts the search pattern to the end of the line:

:.,$s/:$/;/

This would change all end of line occurrences of **:** into **;**.

Ranges can also be specified by putting them in square braces [], such as **[a-z]** for all lower case (the − means through), or **[0-9]** means all digits. These patterns can be preceded by characters; **lcs[0-5]** will match *lcs012*, *lcs555*, but not *lcs987* or *lcs601*. The **&** meta-character can be used in the new pattern to reproduce the old pattern:

:1,$s/historic/pre&/

would change all occurrences of *historic* into *prehistoric*.

Most of these meta-characters work with the search command, ie:

/^Let

will search for a beginning of line occurrence of Let. This does not need to be prefixed by a **:** character.

If you wish to use the meta-characters in a normal search/substitution pattern , you must precede them by the **** escape character:

:.,.+5s/\$/£/g

searches for *$* signs and will change them to £ signs. Note the use of relative addressing (**.+5** meaning five lines from the current line). The use of / characters as delimiters is arbitrary, **vi** picks up the first non alpha-numeric character after the **s** and assumes that is the delimiter:

> **:1,$-7s!Jasper!& Carrot!**
> **:.-2,.+12s%wrong%right%**

Saving, Writing, Quitting and Reading

The changes you make within **vi** are not made to the original file. Until you write the contents of the edit buffer the original document remains unchanged. To save your changes and exit **vi** press **ZZ**, or alternatively you can press **:x**. If you have not made any changes and wish to leave, **:q** will quit the editor. However, if any changes have been made to the edit buffer, **vi** will only let you quit with **:q!**. To write the contents of the buffer to another file type in **:w filename**. If we wished to save our global changes into a new file, we could type

> **:w solitude.glb**

and get

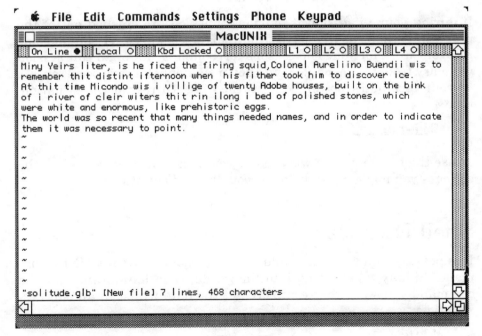

Figure 13

If the file already existed, **vi** would prompt for the form **:w! filename** to overwrite it. Files can be read into the document from the current cursor position with **:r filename** format.

Reading multiple files

More than one file can be read into **vi** at a time. Typing:

%**vi chap.1 chap.2 chap.3**

you will call up **vi** with three file names. **Vi** will open with the file *chap.1*. To exit the current file and read in the next, type

:n

vi will either save the current file or prompt you to save it, and then load in the next file.

Recovering from crashes

If during your **vi** session it happens that you are crashed out of the program without having saved your current changes, **vi** can do some recovery work for you. The reasons for 'bombing' out of an edit session will vary from the machine going down suddenly (a rare occurrence), to your terminal's power being turned off. To rescue the situation, type

%**vi -r chap.1**

or use the file name you wish to recover. This will then save all of the changes you made up to the point you dropped out of **vi**.

Shell Escapes

It is possible whilst in command mode in **vi** to call up any UNIX command. Simply type **:** to go into line mode, then **!command**, for the command you want to execute. To get the date whilst in an edit session type:

:!date

26

Or if you were editing a C program and wished to run it through the **lint** checking program, you could type:

:!lint sort.c

The output of commands can be inserted into the file by using shell escapes followed by a specification of where to place the output.

!!Hdate

will merge the date onto the top line of the screen. The **H** is directing **vi** to place the cursor in the home position before merging the output. The **!!** can be followed by most **vi** cursor movements to specify the text to be used as input for the command. So **!!}** will specify to the end of the paragraph and so on.

It is possible to take some specified text from the file being edited, run a program on it, and replace it with the results of that program. To run the C program beautifier **cb** on the current file, and replace it with the beautified output, type:

!!Gcb

This will only work if you are at the beginning of the file. The **G** command will default to the end of file. So **cb** is being executed with all of the edit buffer as its input, and that buffer will be replaced with the 'beautified' output.

If a large amount of interactive work is to be done, but you wish to remain in the editor, the command

:sh

can be executed. This will run a new interactive shell which will take your command input, until you type **^d** or **exit**. On quitting the shell, control will be returned to **vi**.

Marking blocks

It is possible to mark blocks of text within **vi**. Go to the beginning or end of the block you wish to mark. At the position where you wish to place your mark, type in **m** followed by a character in the a-z range. It is possible to have up to 26 different markers within the text. If you

27

use a marker that has already been used then it will no longer mark the previous place in the text. To go to the marker type

'character

(character being which ever character was used to mark the spot). An alternative usage is:

`character

The **'character** format moves the cursor to the beginning of the line marked, the **`character** moves it to the place of the mark on the line.

The markers can be used for moving and copying blocks of text. Simply mark the beginning or the end of the piece of text required, using the character **x** for example. Then move to the opposite end of the text, and using the **d**, or **y**, command depending upon whether or not you wish to copy or delete the block, followed by the marker **`x**. This will then delete or copy the block up to your marker.

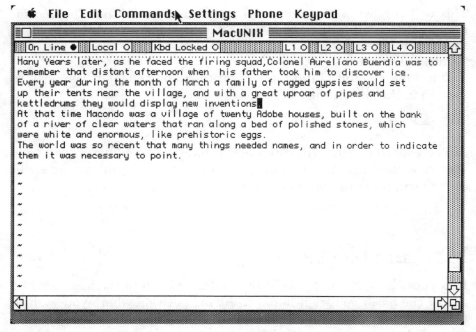

Figure 14

If the section of text beginning with 'Every' and ending 'inventions' had been inserted, in the wrong place. You would need to take the following steps to move it. We would move the cursor to the E of *Every*. In this position we would press **ma** – the use of **a** is arbitrary as any lower case letter would have done. We would then move to the end of the block of text, which is the full stop after the word *inventions*. We can then delete up to the marker, typing

    d`a

This will get **vi** to delete up to the marker. As the marker was on the beginning of the line we could have used

    d'a

We can then move to the place we wish to put the text, in this case at the end of the text and paste it using the **P** command.

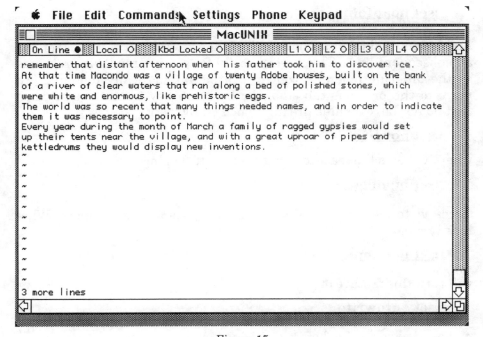

Figure 15

setting vi options

Certain options on how **vi** operates can be reset. To see what options are available whilst in a document, type:

> **:set all**

This will then report upon all settings. These include things such as how many lines **vi** will display, whether or not **vi** will automatically indent lines following tabs, and settings such as how many affected items will cause **vi** to report changes. Most of these settings can be changed. To alter the number of lines **vi** displays to 24, type:

> **:set window=24**

This setting is useful if you are going to use 1200 baud terminal line, as **vi** reduces the number of display lines, to allow faster scrolling and refresh. Other settings such as the auto-indent facility can be set by:

> **:set autoindent**

or unset it by

> **:set noautoindent**

Autoindent makes **vi** automatically indent to the current tab, setting all subsequent lines. This is very useful for writing readable programs as the differing layers of control can be automatically indented. To move to the previous tab stop, the back tab key is **^d**. The settings that do not have a value are all turned off by using

> **:set novalue**

where value is the feature being turned off. Typing

> **:set numbers**

forces **vi** to list program lines prefixed by their line numbers. Whereas typing

> **:set nonumbers**

will turn this feature off.

> **:set autowrite**

makes **vi** save the file before servicing **!** or **:n** requests.

You may find there are certain settings that you use all the time in your **vi** edit sessions. To have to repeat these instructions on the onset of each edit session can be irritating. A far better method is to create a file in your home directory called **.exrc** that contains all these command lines. Then whenever the **vi** or **ex** editors are called they will automatically read and carry out those instructions. A typical **.exrc** file might contain:

> **%cat .exrc**
> **set nomagic**
> **set autoindent**
> **set window=22**

macros

It is also possible to create your own macros for use within **vi** using the map command. For example. If you wished to have a command which added s to the end of word you could type in

> **:map S asESC**

where **ESC** stands for pressing the escape key. Then whenever you type in S whilst on a specified word it will go to the end of the word and append an s. The earlier use of the **cb** command could be made into a useful macro

> **:map B 1G!!Gcb^v^m**

This macro will call **cb** with the entire edit buffer as its input and for its output. The **1G** sends **vi** to the top of the file, **!!G** specifies all of the file for **cb**. The formula **^v** (control v) is used to allow **vi** to insert the carriage return, **^m**, into the macro and not act upon it. This means that the macro will be executed when **B** is pressed, with no need for carriage return to be pressed. Such macros can be specified in **.exrc** files.

miscellaneous features

To change the case of the current character type in ~. This will change lower case into upper case and vice versa. A useful feature when writing C programs, a common occurrence on a UNIX system, is the % command. Typing % upon any of these brackets {} [] () will match up with the corresponding bracket.

Lines can be joined by the **J** command. With these two lines

> **white and enormous,**
> **like historic eggs.**

if the cursor were placed on the upper line, and then J pressed, this would result in

> **white and enormous, like historic eggs.**

ex

You may find that on some occasions it is not desirable or possible to use **vi**. On the UNIX system there are two standard line editors, **ed** and **ex**. It is worth using **ed**, as many other UNIX commands are reworkings of **ed**. However I shall give a brief description of **ex**, as it is similar to **vi**, which is actually based on **ex**, and is powerful and easy to use.

To call up **ex** on a file type

> %<u>ex solitude</u>

The file will either be created or read into **ex**'s edit buffer. You will be prompted with a : prompt. At this prompt it is possible to **a**ppend, **i**nsert, **c**hange and **d**elete text. To get out of text mode back to command mode, and the : prompt, type a . on its own at the beginning of a line. **Ex** can be thought of as pointing at one line of text at a time. To find out which this line is, type

> :.

Pressing return will step you through the lines of the file sequentially. It is possible to use the **p**rint command to see ranges of text.

:1,15p

will display lines 1 through to 15. The rules for ranges and addressing are the same as in **vi**. It is possible to get **ex** to display the line numbers, with:

:1,5£

This would result in

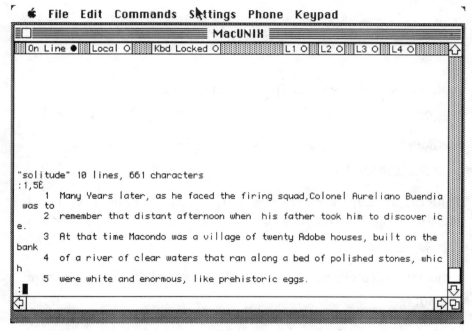

Figure 16

Appending, changing and deleting are similar in **ex** as to **vi**. Moving lines of text is slightly different. Typing

    :6.9 m 45

will move lines 6 through to 9 and place them after line 45, the cursor being left at the end of the new moved text. Lines can be copied in a similar way.

    :47,60 co 0

will make copies of lines 47 through to 60 and place the copies at the beginning of the file. The cursor will be left at the end of the new copied text.

To exit **ex** and save changes made type

    :x

To write the changes to the file without exiting

    :w

The buffer can be written to a specified file name

    :w chapter.1

If the file already exists the format **w!** will have to be used. Leaving the editor without saving any changes, is

    :q

If this means ignoring any changes made to the edit buffer, the form

    :q!

will have to be used. **Vi** can be called up from within **ex**, by typing

    :vi

More Commands

ls with options

In order to find more information about a file type in:

%**ls -l**

FILE TYPE	PERMISSIONS	LINK COUNT	OWNER	SIZE (CHAR)	CREATED (DATE)	CREATED (TIME)	NAME
d	rwxr_xr_x	2	bin	1024	Jan 15	13:00	.
d	rwxr_xr_x	32	root	1024	Jun 1	12:04	..
_	r_xr_xr_x	1	bin	2354	Nov 9	09:34	ar
_	r_xr_____	1	bin	5764	Aug 11	22:00	dd

*Figure 17. **ls -l** output*

The **-l** option gets **ls** to give the user a long listing. A full description of the fields **-l** reports is given in figure 17.

Some of the other options are:

-F which reports directories with a trailing / and an executable file suffixed *.

-t which orders the files by modification time.

-a also reports on . & .. (the parent and current directory),and all files beginning with a '.'.

-r reverses the normal order of **ls**'s output.

-i lists the inumber for each file.

-g shows the group id for files in place of the user id.

Many of these arguments can be combined, ie **ls -rtl** will give a long output reverse sorted by modification time. This is not an exhaustive list - **ls** has 18 different arguments.

chmod (**ch**anging a file **mod**e)

The **ls -l** listing gives the file permissions as three sets of three permissions, commencing at the second character;

-rwxr-xr-- 1 lcs050 12390 Aug 12 1986 12:01 parking_lot

The first character indicates what type the file is: a '-' means a normal file; **d** a directory; **c** a character special file; **b** a block special file; **l** a symbolic link; and **s** means a socket.

So if you changed directory to the **/dev** directory, where all the device files are kept, and typed

%**ls -l**

you would see something like this:

```
brwxr__r__  2  root     1,1 Dec 10  1986  09:00  mt0
........
crwxr__r__  2  root     2,1 Dec 10  1986  09:00  rmt0
crw__w_w_ 1  lcs068   3,9 Feb 2   1987  11:02  tty09
```

Although these files are really hardware devices, such as disks, terminals, magnetic tape drives and so on, they can be treated in most respects like any other file. They can be, in most cases, written to, copied and deleted using the normal commands. Some things don't make sense with certain device files, like reading from a printer for example. However the kernel of UNIX needs to treat them in different ways when it comes to the business of actually getting data from them, or of sending data to them. So the **b** and **c** in the first column shows that UNIX is going to treat them as special files, the b and c standing for block or character. Whether or not they are block or character devices depends upon the nature of the device; a terminal will get its data a character at a time, a tape will read blocks of data at a time. Most block devices also have the capability to be treated as character, also known as raw, devices. The socket is a special file interface for networking. Links will be dealt with later on in this chapter.

The permissions on a file are **r**=read,**w**=write and **x**=execute, and a – character signifies that this permission has been turned off. The three groups are, reading left to right; owner, group and public. The group of a user is determined by the system administrator and is found in the files **/etc/passwd** and **/etc/group**. Public permissions apply to anyone who is not the owner or in the owner's group.

To change permissions. Imagine the 9 permissions, **rwxrwxrwx**, as a 9 bit number. Substitute 1 for a **r,w** or **x** and 0 for **-** . For one of the groups of **rwx** we get:

Pattern	Binary	Octal	Permissions
- - -	0 0 0	0	none
- - x	0 0 1	1	execute
- w -	0 1 0	2	write
- w x	0 1 1	3	write & execute
r - -	1 0 0	4	read
r - x	1 0 1	5	read & execute
r w -	1 1 0	6	read & write
r w x	1 1 1	7	read, write execute

Each category of users permissions are worked out, and then given in full as an octal (base 8) number.

To give permissions **rw-r-xr--** on file *project* type:

%chmod 654 project

```
rw-  r-x  r--
110  101  100
 6    5    4
```

To turn permissions off (mode ---------), type:

%chmod 000 project

Only the owner of a file or the super-user may change the mode of a file. Execute permission on a directory means that it can be searched for named files, which can then be looked at, but without read permission, the directory cannot be listed. Files with write permission may be altered or overwritten completely, however without write permission to the directory, files cannot be deleted or created.

There is also an alternative symbolic mode for changing permissions, this consists of using the symbols:

Symbol	Meaning
u	user
g	group
o	other
a	all
r	read
w	write
x	execute
s	set uid on execution
t	save text

and the operators:

+	add
-	take away
=	assign

So to give the owner and group write and execute permission on a file called **notice.data**, type

%**chmod ug+wx notice.data**

This command will leave the other permission unaffected. To remove write permission for group and others, type

%**chmod og -w notice.data**

To give all categories execute permission, type

%**chmod a +x notice.data**

Assign differs from add in that it leaves the file set only with the permissions given in the command line. So

%**chmod a =x notice.data**

would leave notice.data with only execute permission for all categories. To remove all permissions type

%**chmod a= notice.data**

To specify different permissions for different categories of user, separate each category by comas. To give the owner write permission, the group read permission and all other execute permission, type:

%chmod u+w,g+r,o+x notice.data

The last two permissions that can be granted, set user id on execution and save text are two special permissions. The set user id allows whoever executes the program to take on the user id of the file's owner. So if I run a file owned by root, with set user id permissions effective, for the duration of the execution of the program, I have root's id and therefore root's permissions. The main use of this is to allow limited and program supervised access to restricted parts of the system.

The **passwd** command is a good example of an application for set user id. All users need to be able to change their passwords every now and again. For security reasons write access to the password file, **/etc/passwd**, has to be limited. We have a quandary, how to maintain security and allow users write permission to the password file?

Using set user id permissions is the way out. The **passwd** command is set user id, so that while users are running the program they have super-user permissions,as root owns the file. This gives them write permission to the password file, however this access is limited to what **passwd** will allow users to do, namely change their own password.

The existence of set user id programs owned by root, or any other privileged users is a potential disaster for security. Programs that have set user id must be very limited, and must be well written. If any program which allows a user to execute another command through it, were made set user id, then the system becomes wide open. Any user could then run a shell, a command line interpreter, which would then have root's permissions and could do anything with the system they wanted - change permissions on the password file, reformat the disks and so on.

The save text option is used to attempt to make the system more efficient. It is normally set on popular commands such as editors, compilers etc, and it means that UNIX will attempt not to swop out the text of the program, the instructions, unless it has to. This means that other people trying to execute the program should have a better chance of finding it in main memory. Thus saving the operating system all the time of locating the file, loading it, and swapping out other files.

To set the user id mode on a file only user or group user categories can be specified. Setting the user id for group, setting group id, allows users executing the program to take on the group id of the file. To set user id on a file type:

> %**chmod u+s notice**

or

> %**chmod 4755 notice**

The file permissions will look like this, with an **s** in the place where the **x** for execute permission was:

> **-rwsr-xr--1 lcs068 47822 Jan 12 1987 12:01 notice**

To set the save text bit on a file either type:

> %**chmod a+t notice**

or

> %**chmod 1755 notice**

more

More is used in preference to **cat** for looking at long files;

> %**more /etc/passwd**

more will stop a screen full at a time. To see the next screen press space bar, to see a single line at a time press return. **more** has its own on screen help menu. To see this press **h** at the 'more ' prompt.

```
***************************************************************
```

Most commands optionally preceded by integer argument k. Defaults in brackets.
Star (*) indicates argument becomes new default.

```
-------------------------------------------------------------------------
```

<space>	Display next k lines of text [current screen size]
<return>	Display next k lines of text [1]*
d or **ctrl-D**	Scroll k lines [current scroll size, initially 11]*
q or **Q** or **<interrupt>**	Exit from **more**
s	Skip forward k lines of text [1]
t	Skip forward k screenfuls of text [1]
`	Go to place where previous search started
=	Display current line number
/<regular expression>	Search for kth occurrence of regular expression [1]
n	Search for kth occurrence of last r.e [1]
!<cmd> or **:!<cmd>**	Execute <cmd> in a subshell
v	Start up /usr/ucb/vi at current line
h	Display this message
ctrl-L	Redraw screen
:n	Go to the kth next file [1]
:p	Go to the kth previous file [1]
:f	Display current file name and line number
.	Repeat previous command

```
-------------------------------------------------------------------------
-------------------------------------------------------------------------
```

The more help menu.

cp (<u>c</u>o<u>p</u>y files)

cp copies files or file hierarchies. The general form is

> **%<u>cp oldfile newfile</u>**

Whole directories can be copied with a wild card character *. If the second parameter is a directory name then the file(s) are copied into the new directory retaining their old name

> **%<u>cp important/* backup</u>**

However only the names of sub-directories will be copied and not their contents.

Directory hierarchies, directories and their sub-directories, can be recursively copied to another section of the directory structure using the **-r** option. The second parameter must be a directory

%cp -r bigdir anotherbigdir

Directory hierarchies can also be copied using the **tar** command. **Tar** is the tape archive program and is normally used for copying parts of the system onto magnetic tapes or floppy discs. It can also be used copying from any source onto any target. It also may have less hang-ups about copying over different logical file systems than **cp** does.

mv (__mov__e a file)

mv effectively renames a file or moves it within the directory hierarchy

%mv oldname newname

really only renames **oldname** into **newname**. Whereas

%mv pascal/account.p cobol/bogus.cbl

not only renames the file but moves it as well. If the second file name - **bogus.cbl** - were omitted, then it would be moved without a name change. The contents of whole directories can be moved around the directory hierarchy using **mv**. Using the **-i** option forces **mv** to be interactive, and it will prompt you before overwriting any existing files.

*** *caution moving a file onto an existing file will delete the original* ***

42

ln (linking files)

The **ln** command makes a linked version of a file

%ln pride prejudice

will result in both file names pointing to the same data. The **ls -l** command shows that both files are exactly the same except for their names:

%ls -l pr*
```
-rwxr-xr--2 lcs068  19820  Dec181986  12:01prejudice
-rwxr-xr--2 lcs068  19820  Dec181986  12:01pride
```

Any change made to either file will be reflected in the other file, as the file names are only pointers to the same file information. If a linked file is deleted the data still remains accessible through the other links. Deleting a file from UNIX is really just removing the last link, this also has the pleasant side effect of reclaiming the disk space. The link count is reflected in the output of **ls -l**. A file cannot be linked across two file systems without the **-s** (symbolic linking) option being used. (see chapter 5).

rm (remove a file)

rm removes a file name from the directory structure and if it is the last link, it makes that file index, known as an i-node, and its data, unavailable. For example

%rm unimportant

will remove the file name **unimportant** and, if there are no links to **unimportant**, make the data unavailable.

To remove files you need to have write permission on a directory, as a file is really only an entry in a directory. If you do not have write permission for the actual file, **rm** will prompt you from the standard input, asking whether you really want to remove it. Only the input **y** will result in the file being deleted. The **-r** option applied to directories will recursively remove sub-directories and files within them. This option should be used with extreme care. The command

%rm -r *

will result in all your files being removed – and there is no way of recovering them from within the system and they can only be retrieved from a previous system dump.

mkdir (__ma__k__e__ a __dir__ectory)

mkdir makes new sub-directories, and it accepts a directory name, or path-name, as its argument

> %__mkdir pascal.notes__

will make a directory called pascal.notes with permissions 755 in the current directory. In order to make a sub-directory you have to have write permission to the current directory.

rmdir (__rem__ove a __dir__ectory)

rmdir removes directories from the file system, and it accepts a directory name, or path-name, as an argument.

> %__rmdir pascal.notes__

will remove the directory pascal.notes. **rmdir** will only remove empty directories. If pascal.notes had any files in it **rmdir** would complain and abort. Directories must be emptied using **rm**, or can be deleted, with **extreme care**, using **rm -r** .

The File System Layout

We have already seen that UNIX treats everything as a file. We shall now move on to see how this has been implemented using i-nodes.

UNIX systems are made up of a series of file systems. A file system differs from a collection of data by the way it is organised. A set of files saved onto a magnetic tape is different from a file system. The user can only find out the names of the files, or read them into a directory, by using the **tar** command. **Tar** is the tape archive command. As UNIX treats all files in an uniform manner, and the tape driver is only a directory in **/dev**, it is even possible to use the **cp** command. However the files can only be accessed sequentially, and in the order they were put onto the tape. There is no hierarchy, as the files are not organised into a directory system.

Likewise the only protection offered would be to deny access to the actual device, by turning off permissions in the **/dev** file. So with a collection of raw data the lack of hierarchy means that there can be no levels of protection. This means that most commands will not be able to access the files unless they are brought into the file system. So the UNIX file system imposes a structure onto the files, and allows uniform ways of gaining access to those files. All of the commands we have looked at so far have used this structure, and are dependent upon its existence.

In order to have a UNIX system running it is necessary to have at least one file system, known as the root file system, and this is the directory /. This contains, at least, all the commands and files the system needs to bring up UNIX and to bring it up in multi-user mode. If the root file system did not have the directory **/dev** , effectively a software map of the hardware devices of the machine, then gaining access to any hardware would be impossible. In fact without **/dev** UNIX would not be able to communicate with the user bringing the system up as it would not know how to communicate with their terminal ! Likewise without commands from **/bin**; such as **ls**, **cat**, and so forth, there is little of a worthwhile nature that a user could do.

45

Other file systems can be mounted, using the **/etc/mount** command, onto the root file system. New file systems are mounted onto ordinary directories in the root file system. UNIX takes care to map the new file systems onto the directories, so that the user is unaware when changing into those directories that she is doing anything special. Until a file system, which will be some physical device partitioned in a particular way, is mounted, its contents are inaccessible to the majority of UNIX commands. There are some commands which will not expect a structured directory system, and can read the raw data in from the disk.

The uses of storage devices as mountable UNIX file systems are unlimited, and it is possible to run file systems from floppy disks, and even tape drives. The only problems can be that the boot and super blocks, as well as the other information that the file system needs, will leave little room for actual files, and with slow sequential access devices the access time will be very poor.

The layout for all file systems, root and non root, is the same. See figure 18. Block zero is the boot block and will contain the system boot strap. This will contain a piece of code that is used to start the system up. On non root systems it can be empty. The next block, number 1, is the super block. There is one super block for each file system. The super block contains information about the size of the file system, how many i-nodes and data blocks it has, and pointers to the free i-nodes and free data blocks. A copy of the super block for each mounted file system will be held in main memory, and this in-core copy will have to be synchronized with the disc copy. The in-core a disk copy of the super block can conflict with the disk version if the machine crashes during some operation on the file system. So if a file has just been created, but the disk version of the super block does not have that entry, then there will be a problem of inconsistency between the super

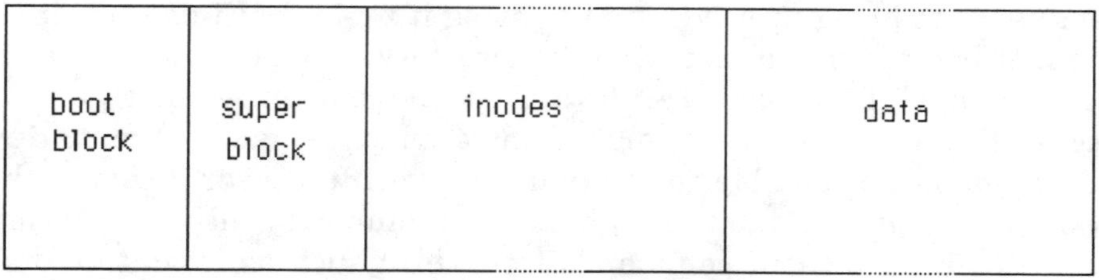

boot block	super block	inodes	data

Figure 18. The layout of the UNIX file system

inumber
rwx mode
number of links
user id of owner
group id of owner
file size in characters
time file last read
time file created or last written
time i-node last changed

Figure 19. A UNIX i-node

block and the state of its data. The program **fsck**, the file system consistency checker, can be run on particular file systems to check if there are problems and attempt to repair them.

The next section of the file system is the i-node list. The i-node list is split into two, used i-nodes and free i-nodes, with the super block maintaining pointers to the free i-node list. The i-nodes are pointers to data blocks and indirect pointers to data blocks. The i-nodes also contain information about what kind of file the i-node is pointing to, for example whether it is an ordinary file or a directory. The i-node contains all the information on the ownership of the file, what permissions it has set and various times regarding the creation, modification and reading of the file.

The i-node also has pointers to data blocks which will contain the actual file data. The size of the i-node, the pointers and the data blocks will be implementation dependent. I-nodes are often 64 bytes, with 4 byte pointers and data blocks of between 1/2k, 4k and 8k bytes. The first ten pointers, 0 to 9, will point directly to data blocks. So on a machine with 1k data blocks these pointers can reference 10k bytes. If these pointers do not reference enough memory the eleventh one points to a further indirect block of pointers. If the blocks are 1k and the pointers are 4 bytes, then this will allow 1024 /4, 256 pointers, allowing 256k bytes of memory addressable. If this indirect block does not allow enough memory then the next block provides a pointer to a block with 256 pointers to indirect blocks. This will give 256 * 256 * 1k addressable data blocks. If this is still not enough there is a pointer to a triple indirect block which has a pointer to a block of 256 pointers to double indirect blocks. This gives 256 * 256 * 256 * 1k addressable data blocks, allowing 16 giga bytes of memory. See figure 20.

How does this relate to the directory structure?

In order to show this let us look at the **ls** command. **Ls** simply reads a directory file or through the i-nodes of files. An **ls** issued without any parameters will simply print out the contents of the current directory, and this means printing out the contents, the data, of a directory file. Issuing an **ls -l** causes **ls** to take each file from the directory, and then get the information from that file's i-node. Different options to **ls** will give different permutations of the information in the i-node.

As with the super block, the kernel keeps in core copies of the i-nodes. These will contain state information about whether the file is being used by a process, whether it has been modified and so on.

There is a price to pay for all this indirection. The work involved in fetching blocks which then point to blocks which point to blocks can be quite heavy. The extent of this problem will depend upon particular machine usage. The Berkeley 4.2 BSD system has attempted to overcome this by providing much larger data blocks of 4 and 8k, therefore meaning that the direct pointers can access much larger blocks of data. This generates another problem. A large amount of memory can be wasted by internal fragmentation, by files leaving large sections of blocks unused. For example a 9k file could, as a worst case, leave 7k unusable. Another suggestion has been to increase the size of i-node so there can be more direct pointers to data and, in some cases, actual data in the i-node.

The next section of the file system is the data blocks, where the data of files is kept. As with the i-node list the data is split into used and free data blocks.

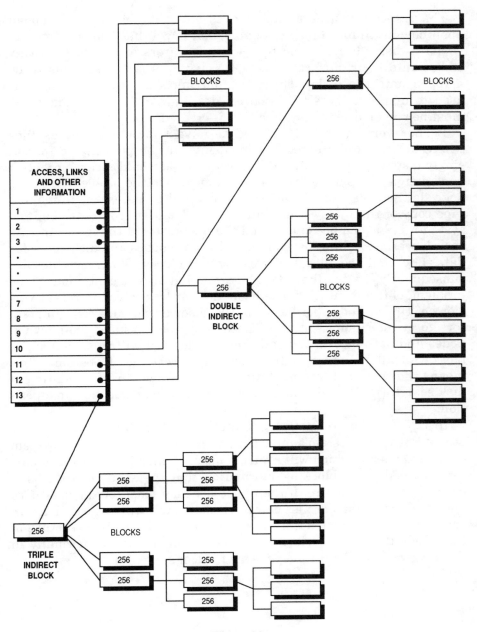

Figure 20

49

The respective sizes of the i-nodes and data blocks will depend upon how much memory is available, and how it has been configured. As hard disks do not come from manufacturers with UNIX already etched into their surfaces it is necessary for the file systems to be mapped onto the disks. The command **mkfs** (make file system) is used to map out the size of the i-nodes and data blocks, and **mkfs** must be run on each file system that is created.

Earlier versions of UNIX used to have a problem that as files where deleted and created the i-nodes would be pointing to increasingly disparate areas of disk. Accessing a file would mean more disk head activity for smaller amounts of data. When the problem began to degrade the operation of the system it would be necessary to make a tape copy of the file system, unmount it, delete its contents. The file system would then be remade and the files restored the from tape. As the file were read into the system and given i-nodes and disk space for data they would be allocated in contiguous blocks. When new files are subsequently created their data blocks would also be contiguous. This problem, of fragmentation, has been more or less solved in recent versions of UNIX. The super blocks in these newer versions contain pointers to cylinder super blocks. These super blocks have their own i-nodes and data blocks, thus all i-nodes allocated within such a super block can all be accessed from the same read head position. This means that internal fragmentation will not cause any degradation of disk search time, as all the data can be accessed from the same position.

In UNIX there are many system calls that allow the programmer access to the file system's information. For example there is a system call, named **stat**, which will return a block of information about a particular i-node. The block of information that the **stat** call returns is defined as a C structure. If the i-node does not exist, or the user does not have the right permissions to read it, **stat** will return -1 as an error message. The structure that stat returns, and the structure of the i-node itself is described in the C header file stat.h, normally in the directory **/usr/include/sys**. This file looks like:

```
struct stat
{
    dev_t   st_dev;    /* device of i-node */
    ino_t   st_ino     /* i-node number */
    short   st_mode    /* mode bits */
    short   st_nlink   /* number of links to file */
    short   st_uid     /* owner's userid */
    short   st_gid     /* owner's group id */
    dev_t   st_rdev    /* for special files */
    off_t   st_size    /* file size in characters */
    time_t  st_atime   /* time file last read */
    time_t  st_mtime   /* time file last written or created */
    time_t  st_ctime   /* time file or i-node last changed */
};
```

The C structure is very similar to a Pascal record and it is used for storing diverse types of information. Most of the entries are self explanatory. The types time_t and dev_t are user defined types that are defined in the file **types.h**. They are user defined types, as the size of these entries are system dependent. St_mode is set to the particular bit pattern which defines the file's mode. These patterns are defined in the file **stat.h** as symbolic constants such as S_IWRITE for write permission, S_IFDIR for directories etc.

In order to use the **stat** system call you need to declare a stat structure, so **stat** has somewhere to dump the information it returns. **Stat** is called with the name of the file that the query is about and the address of the structure. Here is an example piece of code:

```
............
struct stat sbuf;
char *name="myfile";
...............
if ( stat(name,&sbuf) != -1 )
        printf("Group id is %h ",sbuf.st_gid);
..................
```

The line **struct stat sbuf** , is declaring a variable **sbuf** which is of the type structure stat. The **stat** system call is used with a file name and the address of **sbuf** (the form **&sbuf**). **Stat**, if successful it will fill **sbuf** with the information about the i-node. The format **sbuf.st_gid** is looking at individual items of information in the structure.

51

There are other low level system calls to manipulate files and files' i-nodes. There are ones to create, modify and update file data, these are the **open** and **creat** calls. So whenever you issue the **cat** command at shell level, or use a high level language call, such as **fopen** in C, they all have to use the system call **open** to get the information from the file.

Similarly anything creating a file on a UNIX system will have to use the **creat** call[2]. Others deal with linking file names to i-nodes, such as **link** and **unlink**. Usage of the unlink system call on directories is restricted through the command **rmdir** and **rm** with the **-r** option, as unwise use of it could lead to the unlinking of directories that still have files in them. This would leave the file system in a mess as some i-nodes would be taken up and yet have no place in the file system. This situation can occur when hardware faults corrupt directory i-nodes. The command **fsck**, the file system consistency checker goes around the i-nodes looking for 'orphaned' files and links them into the directory **/lost+found**.

So what happens when a user issues a command that deals with a file ?

First we must look and see what the inside of an actual directory file looks like. Although commands like **cat** and **more** will not allow users to look inside directories, commands like **od** and **strings** have no such scruples. The output from **od -c**, octal dump interpreted as characters, will vary from version to version of UNIX. Edition 7 and System V UNIX have a standard format for directories in which the i-node number (inumber) is followed by 14 character file names. The name is padded with nulls if shorter than 14 characters or truncated if longer. Other versions of UNIX allow variable length file name, and the directory will therefore contain the file name length and a pointer to the next entry. The output of

---

[2]The **creat** system call, yes it is spelled like that, has been superseded by the newer versions of the **open** call which allows parameters to create files. However it has been left in to maintain compatibility with earlier versions of UNIX.

%od -c /usr/files/craig

on an Edition 7 or System V machine would look something like this:

```
0000000 312 ( . \0 \0 \0 \0 \0 \0 \0 \0 \0 \0 \0 \0 \0
0000020 243 + . .. \0 \0 \0 \0 \0 \0 \0 \0 \0 \0 \0 \0
0000040 543 * a . o u t \0 \0 \0 \0 \0 \0 \0 \0 \0 \0
0000060 499 = c o r e \0 \0 \0 \0 \0 \0 \0 \0 \0 \0 \0
```

The first two bytes are the inumber of the file and this is the only connection between the file name and any other information held by the system on the file. The **od** command can be used with the **-d** or **-x** to give decimal and hexadecimal output respectively, **od** given without any parameter gives octal output. The inumber of a file can also be discovered by using **ls** with the **-i** option.

If a command like **cat** or **more** is being used then the system must go to the i-node and find out the permissions on the file to check whether or not the user has the correct permissions. When a full path name is given, each of the directories in the search path is checked, and then finally the i-node of the file itself is checked.

As the inumber is the only connection between the file name in the directory and the file's i-node, then it is easy to see how links are made. Obviously an i-node must exist for a link to it to have any meaning. The **ln** command simply places a new name and the existing inumber into a specified directory and ups the i-node's link count by one. So the names of the files are different but they point to the same information, through the same i-node. For example:

%ls -il
12906_rw_rw_r__ 1   lcs068   587   22 Dec   14:08 crime

%ln crime punishment

%ls -i
crime 12906
punishment 12906

%ls -l
_rw_rw_r__ 2 lcs068   587   22 Dec 14:09 crime
_rw_rw_r__ 2 lcs068   587   22 Dec 14:09 punishment

Note that the only change is in the link count for the original file. Any change made to a file is reflected in its links:

```
%echo '"' >punishment
%ls -l
_rw_rw_r__ 2 lcs068   0   22   Dec 14:10 crime
_rw_rw_r__ 2 lcs068   0   22   Dec 14:10 punishment
```

All links are treated the same, there are no privileged links. The **rm** command does not remove , or unlink, i-nodes, but reduces their link count by one. So:

```
%rm crime
%ls -l
_rw_rw_r__ 1 lcs068   0   22   Dec 14:08 punishment
```

When the link count goes to zero, ie the i-node is not linked to anything on the system, the kernel then places that i-node onto the free i-node list and places its data blocks back onto the free data blocks list. **Rm** also zeros the i-node in the directory causing that slot to become free to be reused:

```
%rm punishment
%ls
%od -c .

0000000 817 & . \0\0\0\0\0\0\0\0\0\0\0\0\0\0
0000020 988 * . . \0\0\0\0\0\0\0\0\0\0\0\0
0000040 0   0  c  r  i  m  e \0\0\0\0\0\0\0\0
0000060 0   0  p  u  n  i  s  h  m  e  n  t \0\0\0\0
```

Linking of files across file systems is also problematic. As inumbers are allocated within a file system it is the file system's responsibility to ensure that i-nodes are not double booked, or both pointing to the same data etc. Files that are linked across file systems will not be able to make such checks and know whether or not a particular inumber has already been allocated. If a conflict were to occur then the low level kernel primitives would not be able to locate file or data blocks from an inumber, and all hell would let loose. The **ln** command, on Berkeley UNIX, allows for the **-s** option which provides a symbolic link between file systems. This merely creates a file with the path name of the file linked to. The **df** command shows which file systems are mounted, and where:

54

```
%df
filesystem    kbytes used avail capacity mounted
/dev/win0     4000   3980  20    98%        /
/dev/wina     8000   4000  4000  50%             /usr
```

So linking across a file system creates a new file with a new i-node and inumber.

```
%ln -s /bin/csh /usr/my.csh
%ls -i /bin/csh /usr/my.csh
1425 /bin/csh
9876 /usr/my.csh
```

The **mv** and **cp** commands do something different from **ln**. Copying a file using the **cp** command makes a duplicate copy of the i-node and its data, giving the new file a new inumber. Removing the original makes no difference to the subsequent copies, as they are totally independent both as data blocks and as i-nodes. So:

```
%cp my.csh newcsh
%ls -i
9876 my.csh
1207 newcsh
```

Has created a new, and independent, file called **newcsh**.

The **mv** command has no effect upon the file's i-node and really only manipulates directories. When renaming a file and not moving it in the directory hierarchy **mv** only changes the name, and not the inumber of the file entry in the directory. For example:

```
%mv newcsh notnewcsh
%ls -i
1207 notnewcsh
```

has renamed the directory entry for i-node 1207, from **newcsh** to **notnewcsh**; apart from some information regarding the time this happened, nothing else in the file system is changed. When moving a file within the directory hierarchy **mv** must delete the entry in one directory and write a new one in the target directory. The inumber of the file remains unchanged in both these operations.

To remove a file it is not necessary to own it or have write permission on it. This sometimes confuses users, but it is quite obvious in light of the nature of files. The file is simply an entry of a name and inumber in a directory, the inumber referencing the name to an i-node. To change the directory entry, write permission on the directory is all that is needed. Therefore to delete a file, write permission on the directory is the only requirement.

Deleting sub-directories of files is more difficult. As the user will not have write permission on the sub-directory, and therefore cannot remove the files in it. **Rmdir** will not remove the directory entry, despite the user having write permission in the parent directory, because **rmdir** cannot delete a directory that is not empty. As the directory is owned by another user, the owner of the parent directory may not have write permission, and therefore may not be able to delete the files. Changing the mode of a file owned by another user is not allowed, so without **chmod** the directory is unassailable. Only root can override these constraints, either by deleting files or changing their mode.

Networked File Systems

The above discussion assumes that all of the discs, and file systems, are on the same machine. On many machines it is now possible to have machines which link into file systems on other remote machines. With the development of independent CPU workstations it is possible to have systems which don't actually have their own file systems, but rely entirely on getting their file systems across a network. This requires high speed networking media such as CSMA/CD (carrier sense multiple access collision detect or ethernet systems), as the file systems have to be as responsive as the disc systems they are replacing. It also requires major modifications to the UNIX file system in order to cope with the problems of having them remotely mounted.

There has been the development of many approaches to implementing these network based file systems; Digital developed GFS (generic file system), A.T&T RFS (remote file system), Carnegie Melon University AFS (andrew's file system). The system I intend to describe later on in this book will be the SUN NFS (network file system), and I shall attempt to point out some of the more general networking problems they have had to address.

The NFS system attempts to be transparent, that is the users are not made aware, other than the system being, hopefully, functionally superior, that they are running NFS. This is to allow users the ability to not to have to learn new commands or new forms of pathname. So the semantics for the system, both at user level and at system call level should be the same as on any other standard UNIX system.

The idea behind the NFS system is to extend both the use of the i-node and the concept of mounting file systems. Just as on a stand alone UNIX system, the user is unaware of moving from one physical device to another, for example from one hard disc to another. In the same way NFS extends this by allowing users to move from gaining access to the files on one machine to gaining access to files on other machines.

The SUN NFS system is however only translucent, and it is possible to see the effect of NFS on your files and system; the obvious time that it becomes positively opaque is when one of the machines that is supporting a network mounted file system breaks down and is therefore no longer available. We will look at UNIX networking in more detail in chapter 9.

Some Filters

One of the reasons for the success of the UNIX system has been the quality and variety of useful programs that come with it. These programs are variously known as the filters, utilities or tools. The name filter is derived from the fact that they take some form of text input, filter it in some prescribed way, and then write it out again. The actual ones that any user will regularly use seem to be based on a set of personal preferences. I tend to use **grep**, **awk**, **sed** and **sort** quite a lot, and rarely use **diff**, **comm** or **tr** at all.

grep

grep is part of a family of standard Unix utilities that search files for specified patterns. **grep** actually stands for "general regular expressions pattern matcher" – it matches and reports on patterns. The command:

%**grep 'lcso68' /etc/passwd**

searches the file **/etc/passwd** for any occurrences of the string *lcs068*, printing out each matching line. The use of quotation marks (' ') is not strictly necessary, but they will become useful to stop the shell from interpreting the spaces, and some of **grep**'s meta-characters, in patterns.

It is possible to specify groups of files using the shell's wild card character.

%**grep 'Please type in' *.c**

will search all C source programs, (specified in ***.c** which is the standard suffix for C source programs), in the current directory for the string *'Please type in'*.

58

The result of the search can be changed by specifying certain arguments. The **-n** option gives a notification of occurrences followed by their line numbers.

%grep -n 'goto' /pascal/bad.p

Whilst **-v** inverts the sense of the search.

%grep -v 'wed' /usr/adm/wtmp.list

will only report on lines that do not match the pattern. The **-c** option restricts **grep**'s output to giving the count of occurrences of the pattern.

%grep -c 'lcs' /etc/passwd

will report upon the number of lines containing the string *lcs*. A very useful option is the **-i** option, this causes grep to ignore case differences and match either upper or lower case matches. This is particularly useful when searching for names that may or may not have upper case first characters:

%grep -i 'john smith' /etc/passwd

This would match *John Smith, john Smith, JOHN SMITH* and so on.

Patterns themselves can be made more specific by the use of meta-characters which restrict the meaning of the search. The ^ character restricts the search to beginning of the line occurrences:

%grep '^v9' /etc/termcap
v9 | tvi912 | tvi912c | televideo ....

will only search for beginning of line occurrences of *v9* in the terminal capabilities database **termcap**. The **$** character restricts searches to the end of a line. The command line

%grep -v ';$' *.p

searches all Pascal source files (**.p** is conventional for Pascal files) for lines that do not end with a ';' character. To turn off the effect of these meta-characters they must be preceded by the escape \ (slash) character. To search for the string that begins with a speech mark, type

%grep '\'mistrust' Gotzen-Dammerung
'mistrust all systematizers and avoid them ....

Or to search for a slash character,

%grep '\\' my.script

Ranges within patterns can be specified with **[begin-end]** format. To search for user names in the ranges lcc0nn to lcc5nn:

%grep '^lcc[0-5]..' /etc/passwd
lcc054:*9)^%rrw£op:566:500::/u2/lcc/lcc054
....
lcc555:_+=<mmb&%yt:599:500::/u2/lcc/lcc555

the - character means "through", so 0 through to 5, the '.' character means match any character. Options can be expressed as a list of alternates.

%grep '[A,a]dm' /etc/termcap

will search for occurrences of either adm or Adm. This is different from

%grep '[A-a]dm' /etc/termcap

which will search through the range from A to a and would match Bdm, Qdm and Zdm etc.

fgrep and egrep

There are two more members of the **grep** family, **egrep** and **fgrep**. **Fgrep** is the simplest, in that it is a faster, but more limited version of **grep**. It can only search for literal strings, and can have no ranges or positions specified. If you were to type

%fgrep '^a' /usr/dict/words

you would probably find that it would find nothing. This is because it would be searching for a string **^a**. It would take the search string literally.

Egrep is an extended version of **grep**. The search patterns can be regular expressions of greater complexity. It is possible to restrict searches to particular sets of patterns.

%**egrep '(^lcc.*)(:10:) /etc/passwd**

has two search patterns. Each search pattern is in the parenthesis (). The first search pattern is restricting it to line beginning **lcc** followed by any other characters. The **.** stands for any character, the ***** for zero or more occurrences. The second search pattern is for a ten preceded and followed by colons. Because the two patterns are next to each other make **egrep** only reports on lines that match both patterns. **Egrep** also allows an OR operator, **I** .

%**egrep '(^lcc.*) I (:10:) /etc/passwd**

would match lines that had either, or both patterns in them. Parenthesis should be used to build up more complex search conditions and to ensure the correct precedence of operator. The normal precedence is, from high to low, [], ***+?**, adjacent patterns and **I**. The **+** and **?** operators work in a similar way to the ***** operator. With:

%**egrep 'a*' /usr/dict/words**

the pattern **a** would be matched zero or more times, with:

%**egrep 'a+' /usr/dict/words**

the pattern would be search one or more times, with:

%**egrep 'a?' /usr/dict/words**

the pattern would be matched zero or one times.

<u>sed</u> (<u>s</u>tream <u>ed</u>itor)

sed is a stream editor. Unlike the other editors, **ex** &**ed** the line editors and **vi** the screen editor, **sed** is non-interactive. A stream of text passes through **sed,** a line at a time, and is selected and edited according to the patterns and actions **sed** has been given. **sed**'s input can either be from the keyboard or from a file and the output is by default to the screen but can be redirected into a file. The line

%sed '1.10d' /etc/passwd

is getting sed to **d**elete the first ten lines in **/etc/passwd**. The original file is unaffected by these changes, and the patterns and ranges not matched as well as any transformations, are sent to the screen. The format for **sed** is:

sed [address,[address]] function[s] [argument[s]] [file]

The brackets **[]** mean that the enclosed are optional. So instead of address **1,10** (ie match patterns from line 1 to 10), we could have

%sed '1d' /etc/passwd

which will only match with the first line. Or

%sed '/^lcs/d'/etc/passwd

which has the same effect as **1,$**, as no address range means match all address ranges. The form **/^lcs/** means match all patterns that start with the strings **lcs** and perform the action on them. And

%sed '/^lcs/d'

sed will work upon the standard input if the file name is missing . The original above example is trivial, and could be done more easily using **grep**. However **grep** cannot edit lines of text.

　　sed can do most of the edit functions of a line editor. To substitute text patterns, the line

%sed 's/[M,m]iss/Ms/g' socio.essay >newsocio.essay

performs a global substitution on all occurrences of Miss or miss in the file **socio.essay**. It is necessary to redirect the output from **sed**, otherwise it would shoot past on the screen and be lost. Those who are unsure about the form **[M,m]**, should go back and read the section on creating files.

　　The substitute pattern could have been prefixed by a range

%sed '1.56s/Marx/Karl &/g' politic.essay

which specifies the range of line1 through to line 56. As **sed** works on its input stream on a line by line basis, relative addressing is not allowed

%sed '1,$-15s/Structuralist/Post-&/g' socio.essay2

The form **$-15** (ie 15 lines from the end) is illegal as **sed** will only know when the end of file has come when it has read the last line.

Commands can be read from a script file, using the **-f** argument

%sed -f sed.script chapter.1

sed will read its commands from the file **sed.script** and apply them to the file chapter.1.

sed can also append, insert and change text using

    a\
    text

    c\
    text

and

    i\
    text

formats. The trailing ****'s are to hide the carriage returns from **sed**. All carriage returns, except the final one, in inserted, appended and changed text should be preceded by a **** . This is to maintain the illusion that **sed** is only working with one line of text at a time. For **csh** users the form for **sed** using **a,i** or **c** is:

%sed '/^lcs/i
The following is a Lecturer in CSM. ' /etc/passwd

The double slashes (****) after the **i**, and after all but the ultimate new line , are necessary as the **csh** and **sed** treat new lines in different ways. **sh** user won't have this difficulty as they can run over onto 'new' lines using the secondary prompt ('**>**'). The use of slashes in script files is the same for **sh** and **csh** users. A **sed** script file could contain the following lines:

%cat sed.script

/VMS/a
**NB VMS (Virtual Memory System) is a trade mark of **
Digital Equipment Corporation.
1,$s/UNIX/& tm/g

63

This script appends on the lines following an occurrence of the acronym **VMS** the text **NB .....** If the **c** option had been used, all the matching lines would have been changed to the text, whilst with the **i** option, the text would have been inserted before the line. The last line changes all occurrences of **UNIX** into **UNIX tm**.

sort

sort is the Unix general purpose sorting utility. As with most filters it reads from the keyboard and outputs to the screen by default. If a file name is given then the sort will be applied to it. The simplest sort is to alphabetically order a list of names in a file

%**sort name.list**

This would order the names alphabetically starting from left to right on a line-by-line basis. It is possible to start the sort at a different place in the line. This is done with the form

%**sort +pos1.pos2**

The **+pos1.pos2** is directing **sort** to start from a different record. **pos1** is the number of words across, words being strings of characters separated by blanks and tabs. Words are numbered from left to right starting at 0. **pos2** is further specifying a start position within the word. Both default to 0.

%**sort namelist**

is actually saying **pos1=0** and **pos2=0**, whilst

%**sort +3.2 last.log**

will order **last.log** from left to right starting the third character in the fourth word across. If **pos2** is not specified then it is taken as 0, so

%**sort +2 wtmp.list**

will start at the first character of the third word.
With data in the form:

first_name   Sur_name   Address   'phone_no   age

To sort on the surname field with

%<u>sort +1 company.data</u>

may have unwanted effects. For example when the surnames are the same the sort will go on to the digits of address. ie:

Robert	**Smith**	**10 Landsdown Road**	.....
Anne	**Smith**	**23 Over Street**	......
Peter	**Smith**	**99 Under Ave**	.....

To stop **sort** automatically carrying over onto the next column, the -**pos** form is used.

%<u>sort +1 -2 company.data</u>

will start the sort from column 2 then revert back onto the first column when it has sorted on the second, giving:

Anne	**Smith**	**23 Over Street**	......
Peter	**Smith**	**99 Under Ave**	.....
Robert	**Smith**	**10 Landsdown Road**	.....

Numeric sorts can be achieved using the **-n** option

%<u>sort -n +3 last.list</u>

The **-r** option will reverse the sense of the sort. So if the file numbers contained:

44
1
12
15

it would be sorted:

1
12
15
44

by **sort -n numbers**. Whereas **sort -rn numbers** would produce:

44
12
15
1

The **-o** option specifies an output file. **sort's** output can be redirected as per normal using **>**,

%**sort big.mess >big.sort**

Using the **-o** option allows you to specify the same file for input as well as output

%**sort -o company.data company.data**

AWK

AWK is a pattern scanning and matching language. It is a powerful but ungainly programming tool, and although it is often used as a filter on UNIX it can also be used for more general programming. One should not be put off by the limited documentation and rudimentary error message facilities. This section will give a brief example of using **AWK** both as a useful command and as a programming language.

    AWK breaks up its input into fields and records. A field is separated , by default, by a space or tab character, a record is delineated by a carriage return character. The general form is:

awk pattern(s) { action(s) } file

The input file is read a line at a time. The input is broken into records (lines) and the records are broken into fields (words). The input is then matched against the patterns in the **AWK** program, and the respective actions are performed on the matching input. If no pattern is specified, then every line is acted upon. If no action is specified, then **AWK** outputs each line to the screen. The patterns and actions can be given on the command line, or more commonly can be put into an **AWK** program file, which is read using the **-f** option. The text files by which **AWK** reads its command input from, will always be referred to as programs.

will read the **AWK** program from the file **awkscript** and the input data from **input.dat**. If no input data file is specified **AWK** will take its input from the keyboard. In this section I am going to concentrate on using **AWK** with the **-f** option, and leave command line 'programs' until the section on piping, when they will be more appropriate.

Internal Variables

AWK takes its input stream a line at a time, lines being separated by carriage return characters. It splits each input line into words, each word being separated from the others by space or tab characters. **AWK** numbers each word from left to right, and individual words can be referred to by the form **$1**, or **$4** and so on. The total number of words in the line is kept in the variable **NF**, so if the line has ten words **NF** will be equal to 10. The final word can also be referred to as **$NF**. Note that **NF** is not the same as **$NF**. The whole input line is kept in the variable **$0**. So with the line of input:

The world is all that is the case

The variable **NF** would be set to 8, **$NF** would be '**case**', **$5** would be '**that**', **$0** would be equal to the entire line. There is also a variable **NR** that is set to the number of the current record. On the first line it will be set to one, the second two, and so on. The **AWK** program

{ print NR $0 }

will print out all the lines of a file, each line preceded by its line number. If this were in the file **awk.1** then it could be run using a file **tractatus** as its input by:

%**awk -f awk.1 tractatus**

The fields in a line can be printed out in any order.

{ print $5 $4 $3 $2 $1 }

would print out the first five words of the input in reverse order. The output will not be separated by spaces. To separate by spaces use

{ print $5 " " $4 " " $3 " " $2 " " $1 }

The above programs would be applied to every line as there is no pattern matching done to select lines.

AWK has control structures much like any other programming language. **AWK**'s constructs are syntactically close to those in the C programming language. One such construct is the **for** loop. The general form for the **for** loop is:

for (expression1 ; condition ; expression2)
    action

Expression 1 tends to be initialising a counter, or setting some loop counter, condition is the terminating case of the loop, and expression 2 is normally some increment of the loop counter. An example could be

```
{
for ( i = NF ; i > 0 ; i-- )
    print $i
}
```

This program will print the words in each line of text in reverse order. The value **i** is set at the beginning of the loop to the variable **NF**, ie to the number of words in the current input line. On each iteration **i** is tested to find out whether it is greater than 0, as there is not a zero'th field to access. At the end of each iteration **i** is decremented using the -- operator. This has the same effect as **i = i - 1**. **AWK** has the increment operator ++, which is also unary and has the effect of **i = i + 1**. On each iteration of the loop fields of the input line are printed out in descending order.

AWK also has a **while** loop, so the above program could have been rewritten:

```
{
i = NF
while ( i < NF ) {
    print $i
    i --
}
}
```

Blocks of statements can be bracketed using the 'begin' and 'end' separators { and }.

It is possible to have certain actions only done at the beginning and end of programs.

```
BEGIN   { FS=":" }
        { print $1 }
END     { print FILENAME" has "  NR "lines" }
```

In the above command, the statement after the **BEGIN** is evaluated only once at the start of the program file. This example sets the field separator to a new character, a colon. **AWK** will then treat fields as characters separated by ":"s, which is the format for fields in the password file **/etc/passwd**. The main body of the program prints out the first field. The **END** statement prints out the total number of records (lines) in the file, the variable **FILENAME** is set by **AWK** to the current input file name. If this program were applied to the file **/etc/passwd**, it would print out all of the user's names on the system, followed by the number of lines in the file

%awk -f awk. 2 /etc/passwd

Patterns

So far our programs have not done any pattern matching, and have processed every line of the input files. The simplest form of pattern is matching regular expressions, such as

/lcs/ { print $ }

which would match all lines that contained the pattern lcs, and print out the first field. The match will be made for lines containing lcs anywhere in it. Ranges, and meta characters can be used much in the way they are used in **ex, vi,** and **grep**. To search lines that have words beginning with a particular pattern use

/^lcs/

AWK also provides the control of flow structures **if** and **else**. To write a program to count up the number of users in the group with the group id 500 in the password file. The fourth field of **passwd** contains the numeric group id. The following program would do the job

```
BEGIN { FS=":" }
    {
    if ( $4 == 500 )
        grp++
    else
        other++
    }
END   { print "The group 500 has " grp " members and
        there are " other " others" }
```

Variables are initialised to zero when they are defined. **AWK** is free form with variable comparisons, it will attempt to judge what the most meaningful comparison is. So it can treat variables as strings or numerics dependent upon circumstance.

Ranges can be specified by an [A-Z] format or as alternates in the form [a,z]. **AWK** has relational operators to test certain fields against specified patterns. They are:

Operator	**Test**
==	equality
!=	inequality
>	greater than
>=	greater than and equal to
<	less than
<=	less than and equal to
~	matches regular expression
!~	does not match regular expression

So to test all first words on all lines that are made up only of non-numeric characters

$1 !~ /^[0-9]$/

or

$1 ~ /^[a-zA-Z]$/

The use of ^ at the beginning and $ at the end, makes the pattern match the whole word. Regular expressions must be inside '/' characters, and are constructed like regular expressions in **vi**, **sed** and **egrep**.

Tests can be made using the preset variables.

NF % 2 != 0

matches all lines that have an odd number of fields. An **AWK** program to print out lines with an odd number of fields would be

NF % 2 != 0 { print $0 }

Differing fields can be string compared.

$4 < $5

will do a string comparison of fields four and five. Fields can be string compared with string constants

$6 == "London"

AWK also has logical operators to make up Boolean patterns, they are:

<u>Operator</u>	<u>Test</u>
&&	**logical and**
| |	**logical or**
!	**logical not**

So the test

$2 < '"'   && $7 == "/bin/csh"

will see if the second field is null and test the seventh field against the string "/bin/csh". If the first test fails the second test will not be evaluated.

71

Built in functions

AWK has a set of built in functions , they are:

Function	Does
length(s)	returns the length of string s
substr(s,b,n)	returns a sub-string of string s, starting a position b and n character long. Returns 0 on failure.
index(s1,s2)	reports on the position of the first occurrence of string s2 in string s1. Returns 0 on failure.
split(s,arr,fs)	returns string s split into fields, separated by fs, or if fs not specified, a default FS of blanks is used. The elements can be accessed in the array as arr[1], arr[2] and so on.
printf(fmt,s1,s2..)	print arguments s1,s2 to sn in the format specified by the string fmt.
sprintf (fmt,s1,s2..)	return variable of type created by applying format string fmt to strings s1,s2 to sn.
int(exp)	returns integer value of exp. Rounds down.
cos(exp)	returns cosine of exp.
sin(exp)	returns sine of exp.
log(exp)	returns natural logarithm of exp.
exp(exp)	returns the exponential of exp.
getline()	reads next line of input. Returns 0 on end of file, 1 if not.

Length can be used in two ways. Firstly as a pseudo variable it will report on the length of the current record.

{ print length $0 }

will print lines of input prefixed by their length. **Length** as a function will return the length of the string passed to it. So

length($5) > 80 { print "entry too long " }

will test the fifth word, and print a warning message if it is greater than 80 characters.

Here is a program which checks if the first word on each input line is a palindrome – ie it is the same spelled backwards as forward:

```
{
rev = ""
for ( i = length($1) + 1 ; i >= 2 ; i-- )
{
      tmp = substr($1,i-1,1)
      rev = rev tmp
}
if ( $rev == $1 )
      printf("The string %s is a palindrome\n",$1 )
else
      printf("The string %s is not a palindrome\n",$1 )
}
```

The use of the bracketing forces everything within the brackets to be treated as one pattern, this would allow the program to step through each word of each line:

```
for ( w = 1 ; w < NF ; w++ )
{
rev = ""
for ( i = length($w) + 1 ; i >= 2 ; i-- )
{
    tmp = substr($w,i-1,1)
    rev = rev tmp
}
if ( $rev == $w )
    printf("The string %s is a palindrome\n",$w )
else
    printf("The string %s is not a palindrome\n",$w )
}
}
```

If the bracketing were not used, the first two **for** loops would be done on each line, then the whole input line would be tested against the **if** statement, rather than each individual word of each input line being tested by the **if** statement. The **printf** statement formats the output as well as prints it. The value %s is replaced by the value of the variable **$w** in the output stream. Other formats are %**d** for decimal numbers, %**x** for hexadecimal numbers, %**f** for floating point numbers, and %**c** for single characters variables. As the **AWK printf** is the same as the C programming one, it is possible to look up the details of the **AWK** one by using **man printf**. Most of the details for the C library **printf** will be applicable to the **AWK** one. The statement **rev = rev tmp** is worth noting as in **AWK** string variables placed side by side are concatenated, and no operator like + is needed.

The above program was executed using the system dictionary as its input file by

%**awk -f palindrome /usr/dict/words**

Pattern	Meaning
%d	Decimal integer
%o	Octal integer
%x	Hexadecimal integer
%u	Unsigned number
%e	Floating point with exponent
%f	Floating point without exponent
%c	Single character
%s	Character string
%%	Single % character
%8d	Decimal right justified by 8 spaces.
%-7c	Character left justified by 7 spaces.
%11.3f	Float number of 3 places precision after the decimal point, and at least 20 overall
%.12s	String print only twelve characters

Printf control strings

Below is a program that shows how **printf** can be used to format output. The program prints out a chart of printable ascii characters with their decimal, octal and hexadecimal values.

```
BEGIN
    { printf("\tCharacter\tDecimal\tOctal\tHexadecimal
    \n\n") }
# a null body
END
{ for ( i = 32; i < 127 ; i++ )
  printf("\t\t%c\t%d\t%o\t%x\n") }
```

The program prints out a header, the **\t** characters will be replaced by tabs, the **\n** stands for carriage return. Other control characters can be sent out using **\nnn**, where **nnn** stands for an octal number.

printf("\007")

would print an ASCII bell character and ring the terminal's bell. The back slash can also be used to output strings that would otherwise be taken by **printf** as formatting information.

printf("\\\"")

would print **\"** on the screen. The above program is also interesting in that it has a null body, the **#** character being used to insert a comment. If the program, in the file **ascii.awk**, is executed without a file name for input, as it needs no input

%**awk -f ascii.awk**

We would get the heading printed by the **BEGIN** section, but the program will then hang, waiting for input. Nothing will happen until we press **^d** (control d) to give **AWK** an end of file signal. It will then process the **END** section. It could have been run using

%**awk -f ascii.awk /dev/null**

which uses **/dev/null** as its input. **/dev/null** is normally better known as a place to throw away data, but it can be read and it will always return an eof. The above example shows the difference between **AWK** which is primarily a filter and a programming language like **BASIC**. **AWK** must read from files or the standard input, and it cannot just

75

run programs. It is possible to get over this by using the **exit** command. With:

```
BEGIN
   { printf("\tCharacter\tDecimal\tOctal\tHexadecimal
     \n\n")
for ( i = 32; i < 127 ; i++ )
  printf("\t\t%c\t%d\t%o\t%x\n")
exit
}
# a null body
```

This allows all the work to be done in the **BEGIN** phase and the program is then exited.

Although **AWK** is mainly for text processing, and it works best with streams of input rather than interactively, it is possible to do the sorts of simple programs one would use **BASIC** for. Below is a program that checks to see if a number is prime or not:

```
{
notprime = 0
if ( $1 % 2  == 0 )
     notprime = 1
else
     for ( i = 3; i < $1 ; i += 2 )
     {
          if ( $1 % i == 0 )
          {
               notprime = 1
               break
          }
     }
if ( notprime == 0 )
     printf("The number %d is prime\n",$1)
else
     printf("The number %d is not prime\n",$1)
}
```

This program could either take its input from a file of numbers

%**awk -f prime number.data**

or from the standard input:

%**awk -f prime**

In both cases the program would only test the first number in each line and skip any other numbers on the input line.

The prime program has a couple of interesting features. In order to reduce the number of tests the number is first divided by 2, if this leaves a remainder then we no longer need to test any even divisors, as any even number is divisible by 2. If it doesn't leave a remainder we have finished anyway. So we want the loop to start at 3 and go up in steps of 2, to only use odd numbers. The expression **i += 2**, is the same as the expression **i = i + 2**. **AWK** also allows this C type shorthand notation with other operators: **-=**, **%=**, ***=**, **/=**. These all have similar effects as the **+=** above. So

    x = 10
    x *= 10
    x /= 2

would leave **x** as 50.

In the **for** loop the number is tested to see if it can be divided leaving no remainder. If it can be so divided then it is not a prime number and we do not need to test any further, so the **break** statement forces control to pass to the next statement after the body of the loop, ie to the next **if** statement in the above example. The **break** statement effectively is a restricted goto statement and will jump over any intervening statements.

AWK provides a **continue** statement for use within loops. **Continue** causes the program to jump to the test part of the loop, ignoring any further statements within the loop.

```
for ( e1 ; f_test ; e2 )
{
        ...........
        ...........
        continue        control will jump back to f_test
        ...........
}

while ( w_test )
{
        ..........
        ..........
        continue        control will jump back to w_test
        ..........
}
```

Both **break** and **continue** work within **for** and **while** loops.

Arrays

AWK provides array data structures. The following program uses arrays to count the members of the groups 100, 200, 300 and 400 in the password file:

```
BEGIN { FS=":" }
    {
    $4 ~ 100 { grp[1]++ }
    $4 ~ 200 { grp[2]++ }
    $4 ~ 300 { grp[3]++ }
    $4 ~ 400 { grp[4]++ }
    }
END   { for ( i = 1 ; i != 4 ; i++ )
        printf("Group No. %d has %d  members\n",
            i*100,grp[i])
    }
```

The array elements are subscripted **grp[1]**, **grp[2]** etc. The dimension of the array does not need to be declared before hand as it will be dynamically allocated and its size is only linked to how much memory can be allocated. The elements of the array are initialised to zero. In the above program each element is incremented using the **++** operator. **AWK** will treat it as a numeric array without it having been declared so. The final loop steps through the array printing out the contents of each element.

   AWK can also work with string arrays, the subscripting being the same, but the elements being strings. It is possible to split strings up into arrays using the **split** function. The following beginning section of a program uses these features to do a simplistic check of a date in the form 12/5/87.

```
Begin { d = "31 28 31 30 31 31 30 31 30 31 30 31"
    split(d,rdate)
  }

size = split($1,date,"/")
if ( size == 3 )
{
    if ( date[2] > 0 || date[2] < 12 )
    {
        month = date[2]
        if ( date[1] < 01 || date[1] > rdate[month] )
            $1 = "An invalid date "
    }
}
else
    $1 = "An invalid date"
printf("The date is %s \n", $1 )
}
    ......
    ......
```

The **BEGIN** section of the program set up a string to all the number of days in each month. This is then split into the array **rdate**, the function **split** uses the default separator, blanks. The second call to the function **split** uses slashes to decide where to split the variable **$1**. The number of elements is returned into the variable **size**, if it is not equal to three then the date must be incorrect. The elements are then checked to see if they are within the range 1 to 12 for months. If they are it is then they are checked to see if the number of days is correct. The third **if** statement uses the variable **month** as an index into the array **rdate** to make sure that the number of days in the first field of the array is within bounds. If the date is incorrect the program resets the field to the message **An invalid date**. Any of the fields from a line can be re-assigned.

Perhaps more interesting is that **AWK** allows associative arrays. This is where rather than using a number to subscript an array, one can use any other value. The **last** command produces system accounting information about when users logged in, how long for, on which day etc. If the output from the **last** command was redirected into a file called **last.data** it would look like this:

who	tty25	Mon Feb 9	12:32 - 12:32	(00:00)
lccops	console	Mon Feb 9	12:30 - still logged in	
mc3036	tty18	Mon Feb 9	12:29 - 12:30	(00:01)
lcs068	tty04	Mon Feb 9	12:28 - still logged in	
who	tty27	Mon Feb 9	12:22 - 12:22	(00:00)
....				
....				
bt3174	tty26	Wed Feb 4	19:05 - 19:06	(00:01)
bt3167	tty27	Wed Feb 4	19:03 - 19:09	(00:06)
mc3005	tty11	Wed Feb 4	18:24 - 08:57	(00:32)

The following program counts up the number of times a user logged for the period of the **last.data** file, and also produces a total of the number of logins per day. As a new user name is encountered an array element is initialised to one, the subscript of the array being the user's name. As subsequent occurrences of the name appear, the element of its name is incremented.

```
{
user[$1]++
day[$3]++
}
END
{
for ( u in user )
        printf "User %s %d times\n",u,user[u] | "sort -rn+2 "
for (d in day )
        print " %d logins on %s\n ",day[d],d | "sort -rn "
}
```

So on the first iteration of the loop we would have:

```
user[who]++
day[mon]++
```

The format:

```
for ( u in user )
```

is the way to access associative arrays in **AWK**. The elements will be given as output in a very disorganised way, as a hashing technique is used to store them. Therefore the output is piped into the **sort** command which orders them into descending numeric order of the number of logins. It is possible to redirect from within an **AWK** script to a file:

printf "%d logins on %s\n",day[d],d >> "last.info"

This will append the output from the print command to the file last.info. The use of parenthesis is necessary for both piping and redirection. However you will note that it is optional for the **printf** statement.

With the program in the file **count** and called by the line:

%awk -f count last.data

it would produce the following output:

158 logins on Thu
85 logins on Fri
46 logins   on Mon
124 logins on Wed
23 logins on Sun
4   logins on   Sat
User who 38 times
User lcs068 26 times
....
....
user mc3099 1 times
user bt3163 1 times

Getting Help

help

Perhaps the first thing to note about Unix's help system, is that it is not terribly friendly. A big problem is that the command **help** is for people doing complex system work. **help** is useless unless you are at that stage.

apropos

If you need to use a command but cannot remember its exact name, you can use **apropos** to find it out. If you wanted to copy a file but you cannot remember the command, type in

%**apropos copy**

Apropos will check a database of command names and short descriptions. If your keyword occurs anywhere in the description, **apropos** will report it. The output from the above is something like this:

arff,flcopy (8 arff) - **Archiver and Copier for floppy**
bcopy (8 bcopy) - **Interactive block copy**
cp (1 cp) - **Copy files**
dd (1 dd) - **Convert and copy a file**
....
....
uucp,uulog, uuname (1C uucp) - Unix to Unix Copy

The first column gives the actual command name(s), the second gives a brief description. Obviously the more precise you are with the keyword, the less redundant information you will have to read. If you type **apropos a**, you will have to read a lot of lines to get what you want (649 entries on my system !).

man (on-line **man**uals)

To get more information on a command you can use the **man** command. The words in the brackets given by **apropos** give you the manual entry heading. So for the above example we want a file copying program, which **apropos** assures us is **cp**. For further information, type

%**man cp**

This will give a fairly lengthy description of the command, its syntax and any other 'special considerations' (bugs). The **man** command uses **more** for its display, so the rules for seeing pages is as with **more**. If you want information on the manuals type

%**man man**

The number in the **apropos** output, **(1 cp)**, relates to the actual volume of the manual entry. There are 8 volumes on-line, and some entry titles are duplicated. **man** searches the most useful manuals first; ie volume 1, the general user commands . If you want information on the **time** command, type

%**man time**

This will report on volume 1's manual entry. If you wanted to see the entry in volume 3, the libraries volume, type

%**man 3 time**

To find out what is in each volume you can type

%**man n intro**

where **n** is the number of the volume you are interested in. The different volumes are:

Volume	Subject
one	general commands
two	system calls
three	library routines
four	system files
five	miscellaneous
six	games
seven	hardware, networking & special files
eight	system maintenance

whatis

So **whatis copy** will report that copy is not found, as it is not a command name. Whereas

> %<u>**whatis cp**</u>

will give a brief report on what **cp** does.

whereis

Whilst **whereis** is not strictly speaking a help command, it does give useful information about commands and manual entries. The line

> %<u>**whereis cp**</u>

will report on the location of the command **cp** and which manual volume it is in, in the form:

> **cp:/bin/cp/usr/man/man1/cp.1**

This is useful for finding the **man** volume number as **apropos** and **whatis** have been known to be wrong! If **whereis** cannot find the command or manual entry it will echo back its argument.

Redirection and Pipes

Redirection

Earlier on we saw how it was possible to redirect input from the **cat** command into a file. On the UNIX system three special files are set up when any user logs on. These files are known as **stdin**, **stdout** and **stderr**. Stdin means standard input and is normally the terminal's keyboard; stdout and stderr mean standard output and error respectively. They are both normally associated with the user's terminal screen.

A correct description of the **cat** command should be that it copies the standard input onto the standard output until it receives an end of file (eof) character , normally control d (**^d**). So **cat** without any parameters will simply take all of the standard input (from the keyboard), and send it, on receiving **^d**, to the standard output (the screen). Typing:

> %**cat > newfile**

will redirect **cat**'s output, which normally goes to the screen, into the file **newfile**. The operator **>** is understood by the shell to mean redirect into. We can see from this how **cat** can be used to concatenate files, in the form:

> %**cat filea fileb filec > result**

which will concatenate **filea**, **fileb** and **filec** into the file **result**. **Cat** will assume that files specified are to be taken in place of the standard input unless otherwise stated.

The output of most commands can be redirected. To put the long listing of your files into a file, type:

> %**ls -la > mydirlist**

The output of **ls -la** has been redirected into the file **mydirlist**. If **mydirlist** already existed its contents would be overwritten. The form **>>** appends standard output to a named file. The sequence:

%**date > dirinfo**
%**ls -la >> dirinfo**

would result in a file with the date at the top followed by a long listing of the current directory.

Sometimes it is handy to throw output away, to redirect it to nowhere. If we wanted to use the command **/bin/time** to find out how long a search of the system dictionary for all the lines containing the character **a** takes, we could type:

%**/bin/time grep 'a' /usr/dict/words > /dev/null**
8.9 real   8.1 user   0.5 sys

The file **/dev/null** is a special bottomless pit, and any output sent to it is thrown away. This means that we can time the **grep** command without having to watch all the output on the terminal. The times given are elapsed time (real time), the time spent executing user commands, and the time spent issuing system commands.

Standard input can be redirected in a similar way. If you wished to mail the file **dirinfo** to lcc440 you would type:

%**mail lcc440 < dirinfo**

This redirects the standard input to the **mail** command, which is normally straight from the terminal, from the file **dirinfo**.

Pipes

Doing the sequence:

%**ls -la > dirfile**
%**mail lcsm01 < dirfile**

is a bit slow and means that you have to remember to clean up the temporary files afterwards. What you really want to do is to connect the output of the **ls -la** command with the input of the **mail** command. This is exactly what pipes do. Pipes are used to connect the input of one command to the output of another. Using the | pipe connector on the above example we get:

%ls -la | mail lcsm01

The | connects the output of the **ls -la** command to the input of the **mail** command. So the **mail** command picks up **ls -la**'s output and uses it much in the same way it would if it had be redirected from a file or typed in at the keyboard. If we wished to find out how many users are logged on, we could type:

%who | wc -l

This pipes the output of **who** through **wc -l**, (the **-l** option telling **wc** to only count lines), thus giving us the number of users on the system. Piping most users through the wc is a good idea.

It is now easy to see why the distinction between standard output and error is made. The pipe line gets the standard output, meaning that error messages are still connected to terminal, and thus making sure error messages don't get sent down the pipe lines with the genuine data.

Pipe lines can be fitted up to any length. It is therefore possible to fit together a pipe line of commands and filters.

%who | grep '^mc' | sed '1,$s/^.*$/warning & has logged in/' | mail root

sets up a pipe line which scans the output of **who** for users' names beginning with mc, prefixes and appends the words '**warning .... has logged in**', and mails the result to root. We can now see why it is important for the utilities such as **grep**, **sed**, **sort** etc to read from the standard input and write to the standard output, as this means that they can be used as filters in pipe lines.

There is a special command used for pipe fitting, **tee**. **Tee** splits the input into two, sending one copy to the named file, and the other down the pipe line.

%ls -s | grep '^..[0-9]' | tee /dev/tty | mail adm

will result in all of the files that have block number greater than 9 being sent down the pipeline. A copy of **grep**'s output will be sent to the terminal screen via **/dev/tty**, the other copy will be mailed to the user **adm**. The file **/dev/tty** is used by UNIX as a synonym for the user's terminal, and output sent to it will be sent to the terminal screen. **Tee** can be used to output results of a pipe line into a normal file.

%**last | grep -v 'wtmp' | sed 's/ .*//' | sort | uniq -c |
tee /usr/adm/usage.data | mail adm**

The **last** command reports upon the number and duration of logins of users. **Grep** cleans the final line of **last's** output, which always starts with the word wtmp. This is piped to **sed** where the all but the users' names are stripped off. **Sort** then puts them in order by user-id. **Uniq** counts the number of times a line, and therefore a user name, have been repeated. The **-c** option gets **uniq** to prefix the number of occurrences to the line. This output is then placed in the file **/usr/adm/usage.data** and also mailed to **adm**.

Redirection and pipes at system level

How are redirection and piping achieved ? Part of the UNIX philosophy is that programs do not know, or care, where they are writing to or reading from. UNIX was designed so that utilities could work in a standard way and not have whole series of exceptions depending on where they are writing to or reading from. This means that UNIX utilities can be used in the same way for a wide variety of purposes. So the majority of utilities write to the standard output and read from the standard input.

Redirection

The UNIX kernel is the piece of software that is ultimately responsible for all the details of redirection and piping. The kernel is a program, normally **/unix**, written in a mixture of C and the machine's native assembly language. It is possible to gain access to the kernel through a series of entry points called system calls. These system calls can be thought of as normal external function and procedure calls in a high level language. The calls allow programs and the rest

88

of UNIX access to main memory, and disk storage as well as information about the state of the system. So a user typing in the command

%echo "hello" >hello.file

at the shell, command line interpreter, level is using the kernel system calls indirectly by calling them through the shell commands.

It is worth taking a step back and seeing how UNIX sets up the user's environment. Once running the kernel sets up terminal lines by executing the **init** (/etc/init) and **getty** (/etc/getty) programs. **Init** sets up three files and gives them file descriptor 0,1 and 2, and these are called stdin,stdout and stderr respectively. These files are opened using the **open** system call. The standard way UNIX treats all files can be seen from the fact that UNIX does not need to use any special system calls to create an interactive file for the terminal. However, the kernel needs special pieces of software, called device drivers, to act as an interface between the hardware specific details of the peripheral device and UNIX.

The **open** call can be described in C as:

int open(name,mode) /* open returns an int file descriptor or -1 on error */

int mode; /* access mode for the file, 0,1,2 - for read,write, read & write access */

char *name; /* the path name of the file to be created or accessed */

The **open** call returns an integer file descriptor, normally a number between 3 and 20, or -1 on error. Typical errors range from a misspelt path-name to the wrong permissions on the file or no file descriptors being left. The number of file descriptors per process is defined in the kernel and can be altered by the system administrator.

Init does an **open** on a tty line, one of the files /dev/ttyn, and then uses the **dup** system call to return the descriptors for stdout and stderr. **Dup** returns a duplicate descriptor to a file using the next lowest numbered descriptor available. The piece of code:

fd = open("afile",0);
dup(fd);

will return a file descriptor for afile and a duplicate descriptor, with the next lowest number available. So when **init** opens the tty line as its first file, and then **dup**s it twice it is assured to return 0,1,2.[3]

It is possible to refer to these file descriptor numbers at the level of the shell, specifying to which descriptor redirection is to apply. The Bourne shell is much more flexible in allowing specification of file descriptors, and the following examples of numbered redirection only work under the Bourne shell. Doing:

%/bin/time wc /etc/termcap >termcap.cnt

will still lead to the timings being written to stderr, as '>' means redirect the standard output only. Using the form:

%/bin/time wc /etc/termcap >termcap.cnt 2> termcap.err

will result in the standard error being redirected into a file, **2>** meaning redirect file descriptor 2 into a file. It is possible to refer to any file with the **n>**, where n is a file descriptor, however 0,1,2 are normally the only ones that are referred to in such a way. It is possible also to merge two file streams using

fdn1 >& fdn2

where fdn1 and fdn2 stand for file descriptors. The need to apply this level of precision is commonly seen in shellscripts that are used to boot up and initialise the system. The scripts must be careful to get all the information to the console screen. It is achieved by line such as this

echo ' file system mounted are `/etc/mount` ' 1>&2 >dev/console

This will ensure that both stdout and stderr go to the terminal screen.

Under the Csh it is possible to do the normal redirection of standard input and standard output using **>**, **>>** and **<** operators. The redirection of error output is more limited, though it is is possible to merge the standard output and standard error streams into one file using **>&** :

%/bin/time wc /etc/termcap >& termcap.err

---

[3] Versions of UNIX since version III have a newer form of the open system call which allows files to be created as well as opened, thus making redundant the much loved creat system call. Also the dup system call has been superseded by the fcntl system call.

Independent manipulation of error and output streams as well as redirecting named (actually numbered) streams is not possible under the **csh**.

All redirection happens at the level of the shell. The commands have no idea what is happening to their input and output. The shell simply recognises the redirection operators, **>** **>>** and **<** , and then closes the appropriate file descriptor (0 or 1), using the **close** system call. **Close** stops a particular file being associated with a file descriptor and allows that descriptor to be reallocated. The shell then opens the specified file:

    close(stdout);   **/*close down the output stream*/**
    fd = open(file,2)   **/*open redirect file to write*/**

Like **dup**, **open** returns the lowest numbered possible file descriptor available. As the shell has closed either the descriptor 0 or 1 , the file to be redirected will be opened with that descriptor. The bits of code given are not meant to be serious examples of systems program, as they do no error checking for example, but are used merely to indicate in general how things are done. Thus the programs still write to 1 or read from 0 not realising that these are now ordinary files. The shell obviously has to take care to distinguish whether a process is to overwrite or append to a file and take the necessary action. The shell must also deal with users trying to use files that either don't exist or don't have the correct permissions.

So in a command line like

    %echo 'Hi there' >junk

the command **echo** has no idea that anything is happening to its output.

Pipes

Pipes are a slightly different case though. Unlike redirection, which is simply rerouting input or output, pipes are an attempt to communicate between two processes. The reading end of one process must be connected to the writing end of another. Again all this must happen without either process acting in any different way. So the command line

    %pr *.c | lpr

happens without either **pr** or **lpr** having to act in any special way.

This is facilitated by the **pipe** system call. Which allows a process to set up a buffer that can be written to and read from. The buffer is treated like a file and is accessed as a normal file is. The definition of pipe is:

int pipe(pfd);   /* returns -1 on error */
int pfd[2] ;   /* two dimensional array for reading
                  & writing */

The actual call to **pipe** would look like this

pipe(pfd);

This call would return two file descriptors. These would be associated with the two array elements **pfd[0]** and **pfd[1]** in the above example. The element **pfd[0]** is the reading end of the pipe and **pfd[1]** is the writing end. So issuing writes to **pfd[1]** will place data in the pipe, and issuing reads to **pfd[0]** will take data out.

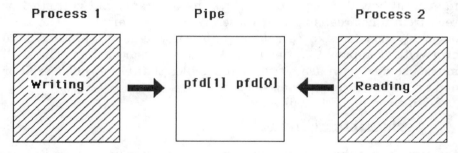

Figure 21. A pipe connecting two processes

Pipes can be treated more or less the same as other files, in that they can be opened, closed, read from and written to. The kernel maintains inodes for pipes, although they are never normally written to disk. There are some things that would make little sense doing with pipes, a seek for example. The bytes are written to and read from in the same order, the pipes are first in first out (FIFO) devices. They normally can buffer at least 4096 bytes. The pipe will act like a normal file and return EOF upon the end of data from the writing end of the pipe.

The **pipe** system call is available to programmers and can be used to allow interprocess communication. However most UNIX users will know pipe from their experience of the shell's piping facilities, and will see little of the wider uses and implications of the **pipe** call. I shall only look at the use of piping from the shell user's point of view.

As with redirection the shell handles all the details and file descriptors of piping. What happens is this. The shell recognises the pipe symbol, the I, in the command line and then attempts to set up the pipe line for the processes. This will involve issuing the **pipe** call which will return two file descriptors associated with two array elements.

For the process writing to the pipe the shell closes down file descriptor one, stdout. The shell then issues a **dup** call with the writing end of the pipe as the file name argument, **pfd[1]** from the above example. As **dup** returns the lowest available descriptor, and the shell has just closed descriptor one, the pipes file descriptor is one, stdout.

```
int pf[2];   /* file descriptors for the pipe */
.........
.........
pipe(pf);   /* set up pipe */
close(stdout); /* close down standard output */
dup(pf[1]); /* open descriptor to pipe which
        will have stdout's descriptor number */
.........
/* then execute the process */
```

The process that is to write to the pipe is then executed, and it will write, as per normal to stdout. However due to the intervention of the shell stdout is now connected to the writing end of the pipe. All the output from the process will now go to the pipe.

The strategy for the process reading the pipe is similar. The shell closes down file descriptor zero, stdin. It then calls **dup** with the reading end of the pipe as its file name argument, **pfd[0]** from the above example. **Dup** again returns the lowest numbered descriptor for the pipe which this time is zero, stdin.

....

....

close(stdin); /* close down standard input */
dup(pf[0]); /* open descriptor to pipe which
will have stdin's descriptor number */

....

/* then execute the process */

The reading process is executed, and it reads from stdin or file descriptor zero, and again the shell has coerced the process into reading from the pipe. Obviously this process can be repeated again and again, with both the writing and reading ends of processes connected to pipelines. The only limitation is the number of open files descriptors and processes on the system.

All of this relies upon programmers writing utilities that do not alter stdin, stdout and stderr. If someone decides to change these three file descriptors, then all bets are off. However there seems little good reason to deviate from this norm and well written programs should check that calls manipulating this 'standard' environment have returned properly.

Communications, File Transfer and Networking

In this chapter we shall look at communications, file transfer and networking under UNIX.

It is said that when two Greeks get together then there will be three political parties; in computer inter-connection this rule is applied to a greater degree. In this section I intend to look at computer communications in three different instances: first, network commands within a network of UNIX machines including using the SUN Network File System (NFS) as an example of a more tightly coupled computer network; second, file transfer between machines with different operating systems; and finally, to look at Local Area Networks (LAN), Wide Area Networks (WAN) and network addressing.

A Common Scenario of machine interconnection

In diagram 22 you will see a simplified schema of the Computer Studies Department computer systems in Bristol Polytechnic. This shows their interconnection as well as their connection to the central machines. The SUN and VAX networks are sub-domains of workstations connected to file serving hosts. All of the UNIX machines are interconnected using SUN NFS.

All of the minicomputers are connected via a thick ethernet cable, the sub-domains use thin ethernet cable. There is a connection through to the JANET network via a PAD (Packet Assembler/Disassembler) which connects to a British Telecom leased line into the JANET backbone. There are serial connections from terminals directly into the mini computers and through terminal servers. Various microcomputers connect into the system either through the ethernet or via serial lines.

BRISTOL
POLYTECHNIC
ETHERNET

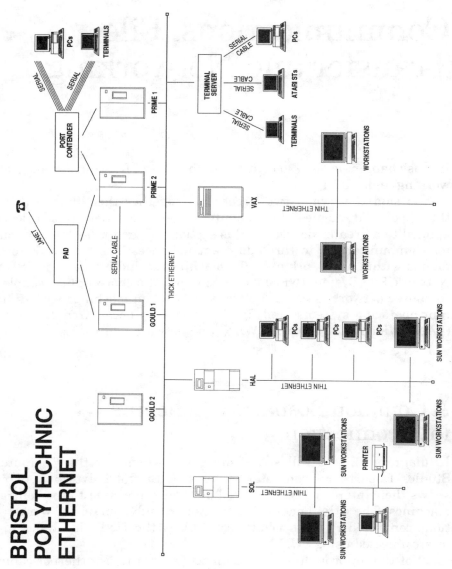

Figure 22

This type of configuration of different machines, operating systems, and media for connection is typical of the type of internetworking that will exist in College departments around the country. The different types of interconnection possible are

- communication within a homogeneous software environment — for example communications between the UNIX machines

- communications between mini-computers over the ethernet for example between the PRIME and VAX computer

- Microcomputer and Minicomputer communication using ethernet and serial cable

- communication with other networks

The details of some of the above communications will vary dependent upon the communication media used. So to connect two minicomputers over ethernet is different from a connection made over a serial line. In the following two chapters I will illustrate how to do all of the above connections.

The International Standards Organisation Open Systems Interconnection

Before we look at the details of communications and networking under UNIX it may be useful to provide a framework for our discussion. The framework or model I shall use is the model for 'open systems' data communication and networking developed by the International Standards Organisation (ISO) and is called the 'Open Systems Interconnection' (OSI).

From the work so far, we can see that, even to our limited level of implementation detail, operating systems are very complex pieces of software. In terms of complexity and implementation difficulty networks are a magnitude more difficult, and, on top of this, they take the traditional problems of operating system design and make them more complex to boot! Therefore a functional model of the network's operations must be capable of breaking down this complexity and making the problems more localised and manageable. A diagram of the ISO OSI model is given below.

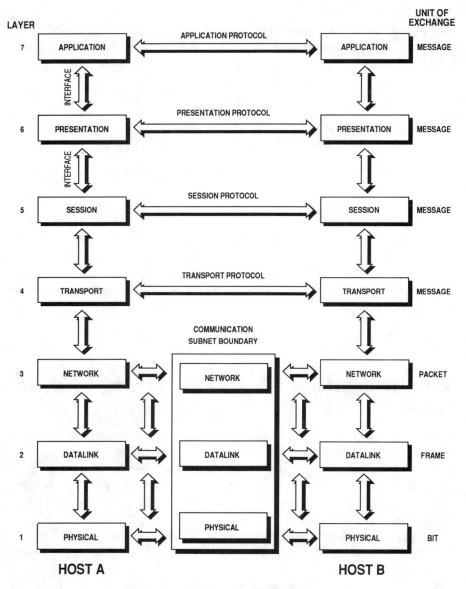

THE ISO OSI MODEL

Figure 23

The ISO model is being developed by government agencies, private companies and academics from many countries under the auspices of the International Standards Organisation. It is meant to facilitate, as the name implies, interconnection between diverse systems from a variety of vendors.

In order to illustrate this let us take an example of a user sending a mail message from one machine to a user on another machine. The user might type in:

%mail lcs050@sol

or something similar. The program **mail** is the **application** that is running at the top level on the local machine. Now if this message were to be sent over an expensive telephone link it would be a good idea to compress the data and thus save money. This is the kind of function that the **presentation** layer would undertake − other functions can include data encryption for security purposes, data transformation (from ASCII to EBCDIC character sets for example). Once the data has been 'presented' it is then passed to the **session** layer. In order for the machines to communicate it is necessary for them to have initialised their dialogue or session. In the current case, with a mail program, the initialisation of the mail 'session' would probably have happened at the same time as the machines were booted up; with other 'one-off' activities the session may be started at the same time as the command is issued. These type of initialisation activities are executed as processes to check incoming messages and supply the correct formats for sending messages out over the network. While the session layer manages the communication the actual work, the sending and receiving of data and so on, is done by the **transport** layer. This layer takes the logical names used by the session layer, **sol** in the above example, and translates them into a lower level address which is less comprehensible to the user but has specific details for the hardware. Now whilst the respective transport layers are sending and receiving data it may well be the case that the message is actually passed between a number of intermediate machines on its journey to the machine **sol**. The routing of messages between various machines is the task of the **network** layer. During our message's odyssey many cruel events can, and will, befall it so error checking along with some repeat transmission will undoubtedly be necessary. This function is the role of the **data link** layer, which, finally places the data, containing all of the control information from the higher layers' additions, onto the actual **physical** medium. It is highly likely that for the message to be processed by the mail application on the remote machine that it will go through the same process in reverse. Phew!

In order for all this to function correctly each layer must harmonise with its counterpart layer on the machine, or machines, it is attempting to communicate with. A set of rules that govern a dialogue are known as protocols; the protocols between layers are known as peer protocols. For example if, in our above dialogue, the presentation layer on the local machine compressed the data using one data compression algorithm and the remote machine used a completely different algorithm then the received message would be corrupted.

In the following discussion we will mainly be looking at the higher levels of the ISO model – we will be spared the gruesome details of the lower network and data link levels, which are implemented in hardware. It is worth remembering that the ISO 7 layered model is a description of a model not an actual working system and UNIX networking actually predates the OSI model by many years. Consequently some of the OSI layers don't exactly match what is happening on working systems – there is even a disagreement about the number of layers that are necessary and their exact function. For example some networks don't have a session layer and all of the session layer functions can be done at the transport layer.

Anyway back to brute reality. The simplest and most common problem for computer users is having a file in the wrong the place. A data file may have been typed in on a microcomputer at home and need transferring onto a mini or mainframe for further processing, or as is often the case, colleagues may all use different machines to type in their documents and it may be beholden upon you to gather them together in one place.

Interconnection of UNIX Machines

We will start our investigation into networking by looking at file transfer and connections between machines that all run UNIX.

Berkeley ARPA Services

Your UNIX system, if networked, will most probably support a set of network services that are collectively known as the Berkeley ARPA Services. These are a set of networking command that seek to extend the semantics of commands for stand-alone UNIX to a networked environment.

rlogin (remote login)

Using the **rlogin** command it is possible to remotely login to machines on the network. It is easy to use

   %rlogin vega

will login the current user to the machine vega assuming that the user has an account on that machine. The remote system may prompt you for a password. It is possible to log directly, without password checks, onto a series of trusted hosts, as long as you have the same username on the remote machine, and that the hosts are included in the either the files **/etc/hosts.equiv** or a **.rhosts** file in the user's home directory. The **.rhosts** file lists the machine name followed by the username for each host on the system. **hosts.equiv** and **.rhosts** is used by the **rlogin**, **rcp** and **rsh** commands.

   It is possible to logon to remote machines with a different username using the **-l** option

   %rlogin -l j saini la louche

This would start the login sequence, including the password prompt, for the user **j_saini** on the machine called **la_louche**. By logging out of the machine, the rlogin session is terminated.

The **rlogin** command has a series of ~ (tilde) escape characters. Typing

%~^z   (tilde control z)

will suspend the **rlogin** session and return control back to the remote host, or if you have remotely logged in through more than one machine, the ~^z will drop control back to the first one. It is possible to quit the **rlogin** session without going through the logout sequence using

%~.   (tilde dot)

Once again this, in the event of multiple **rlogin** sessions will place control back to the first host to issue the **rlogin** command. As with most of these escape sequences the escape character must be the first character typed on a line, any other characters, even if they are deleted, will mask the escape effect of the ~ character.

rusers (remote users)

It is possible to find out whether machines on the network are busy using the **rusers** command. This command effectively does a **who** for each machine, on the network.

```
%33craig @ zugzwang rusers
gould1                   cshroot a_greath tmp50 tmp48 tmp49
la_louche                n_goodwi
zugzwang                 c_duffy
beefheart                wroot
rigel                    a_clymer
gould2                   cshroot cj_watts cj_watts ir_johns
j_saini
sirius                   s_ali
sol                      c_duffy root c_duffy root j_saini
vega                     a_clymer
^c
```

You will notice that the command has to be terminated by **^c** because **rusers** broadcasts its request over the network and does not know how many replies to expect, as machines may be down or unavailable. The normal **rusers** output only lists machines which have users on them, with the **-a** option it outputs all machines regardless of whether or not users are on them.

```
%26craig @ sol rusers -a
sod
gould1
gould2          c_duffy mr_hudso
hal-9000        my arob my gtho jc
sol             c_duffy rob gtho c_duffy rob wroot
centauri
zugzwang        cj_watts
altair
procyon
vega
spica
rigel
arcturus
sirius
la_louche
pollux
crucis
capella
solaris         c_duffy rob gtho c_duffy rob wroot
aldebaran       a_clymer
^C
```

This can be a very useful command for finding a machine that is not being used.

rsh (<u>r</u>emote <u>sh</u>ell)

Quite often you may not need to log onto a remote machine but may only need to do a limited task or set of tasks. The **rsh** command is useful for this situation, this allows the user to run a remote shell command on a nominated machine. So if I wished to do a listing of a directory on the machine **gould1** to see if there was a particular file there I could type

103

```
%28craig @ zugzwang rsh g1 ls -l ~vandals/bus_seats
total 1015
-rwxr-xr-x  1 Ghengis    46809 Aug  3  1990 Khan
-rw-r--r--  1 pj_evans     275 Aug  2  1990 agpeg3.p
-rw-r--r--  1 js_mcall     272 Aug  2  1990 agpeg4.p
...........
.........
```

The format for the command is the machine name followed by the command name. The command names are normal UNIX styled commands, and references to ~ and so on will be referenced to the remote machine. Particular care has to be taken with using piping and redirection, as it has to be made clear which machine's shell you wish to do the piping or redirection. So doing

%craig@sol rsh gould1 who > who_dump

will redirect the output of the **who** command, run on the Gould, into the file **who_dump** on the local machine sol. To remote redirection you must use quote ("") characters to stop the local shell interfering. So

%craig@sol rsh gould1 who ">" who_dump

would create the file, **who_dump** on the remote machine.

It is possible to run remote jobs on machines using only their names, so typing

%vega w

will run the command **w** on the machine called **vega**, these machine name commands will only work if the machine names are listed in the **/usr/hosts** directory, and you have to have the path **/usr/hosts** in your execution path.

Doing an **rsh machine_name** without a shell command is the equivalent of **rlogin machine_name**.

rcp (**r**emote **co**py)

Once you have discovered using **rsh** that a file exists you may wish to copy it across from your remote machine to a local. The **rcp** command is easier than other file transfer programmes such as **ftp**, although, unlike **ftp**, it will not work with non-UNIX machines or UNIX machines which have not had the Berkeley ARPA services installed. To use **rcp** you simply state the source or destination, or both, as **machine_name:path_name**, and as long as the machines, paths and permissions are correct, then the inter-machine copy will take place.

> **%26craig @ vega rcp g1:/golden/horde/Krum Krum**

It is possible to have both the source and destination as remote machines.

rup (**r**emote **up**time)

It is possible to get system statistics about machines on the network using the **rup** command. This gives information about machine load, time since last reboot and so on. It can be used to get a snap shot of the whole network or information on a single machine.

```
%27craig @ sol rup
sod        up 15 days,2:45,     load average: 0.00, 0.00, 0.00
spica      up 4 days,40 mins,load average: 0.09, 0.00,0.00
rigel      up  8 days, 16:17,load average: 0.05, 0.00, 0.00
altair     up  8 days, 16:56,load average: 0.12, 0.01, 0.00
sol        up  4 days, 18:35,load average: 1.17, 0.81, 0.55
^C
```

There is a command **ruptime** which provides similar information. However the deamon which supports **ruptime**, and also supports a **rusers** like command **rwho**, is so enervating of the system, that system administrators rarely run it on their own machines. Finally there is a command called **rwall**, which is a remote version of the **wall** (**write all** users) command. It is unlikely that you will have permission to run this command.

In terms of their relationship to the ISO model, the Berkeley ARPA services cover the bottom 5 layers. This means that users don't have to worry about retransmission on error, routing or the delivery of data. The sessions are set up at system boot-up time, so machines have deamons running which take care of end-to-end communication. However the ARPA services require the user to be aware of the names of machines on the network. They do not provide presentation layer services so there can be conflicts between machines with different architectures.

This can be seen when using the pipe (|) to connect two machines' processes. As the pipe only provides a data buffer between two processes it does not make any allowances for the machines treating the data in different ways. So if one machine were running a program generating floating point numbers, then the pipe could pass them onto another machine. However the other machine may have been made by another manufacturer and have a different processor and architecture. This could mean that it would represent floating point numbers in a different fashion. This would lead to the program reading incorrect data and to the anomalous situation where the two programs would work together perfectly well when run, piping data on the same machine, but would generate strange results when run over 2 machines using a pipe into a **rsh**.

So if the floating point generator was called fwriter and the floating point reader was called freader, when it is run on the Gould we would get

% fwriter | freader
0.000000	1.000000	2.000000	3.000000	4.000000
5.000000	6.000000	7.000000		

But if we tried

% fwriter | rsh sol freader
0.000000	262144.000000	524288.000000
1048576.000000	2097152.000000	4194304.0000

We get garbage as output. This is because the pipe is connecting two different architecture machines each of which has its own floating point number representation. Neither the pipe nor **rsh** is capable of resolving this problem of network data inconsistencies.

Network File Systems

So far we have looked at machine connectivety that is achieved through the user issuing specific network commands. However it is possible for network systems to be implemented that allow resource sharing across machines without the user having to request the resources or even to be aware that networked resources are being accessed. The system I intend to describe is the SUN Network File System (NFS). There are many others, but NFS is one of the most widely available systems around. NFS allows, as its name implies, the distribution of the file system across many machines. This is distinct from distributed processing, where the processing power to execute jobs, or even sub-procedures of jobs, is distributed across many machines.

Designers of systems like NFS have taken as one of their main briefs that the systems should be as transparent as possible. Users should be unaware of the existence of the network and only see the enlarged resources. This means that in order to see how the system works we have to look behind the scenes.

In figure 24 we see two separate UNIX machines, each with its own disc space. Why should we not be able to pool these resources? If for example they are running the same version of UNIX, then we should not need two sets of manual pages on-line. NFS allows this sharing of disc resources without having to change, from the user level, the UNIX commands.

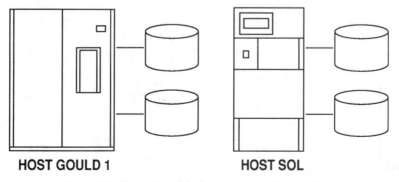

HOST GOULD 1   **HOST SOL**

Figure 24. Hosts having separate non-shared discs

This change has been achieved by major modifications to the kernel, to specific commands and in the file system. NFS has in many ways simply extended the semantics of the **mount** command from one cpu to many. The **mount** command imports disc partitions into the root, the primary file system allowing user access to these files through the UNIX file system. However as each file system mounted has its own inode table and data, it is necessary for the kernel to keep track of which file system it is currently using. As inode 777 in / (the root file system) will be a different file from inode 777 in /usr (the user file system). The kernel maintains information about where file systems are mounted, mount points, and makes sure that inode file references are for the correct file system. The command **df** reports the mounted partitions, plus various statistics about their usage, to the user.

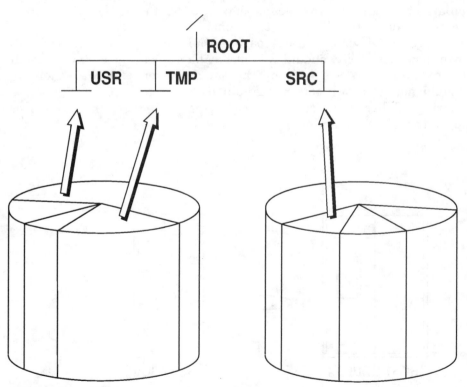

Figure 25. Different disc partitions mapped in the directory hierarchy by mount

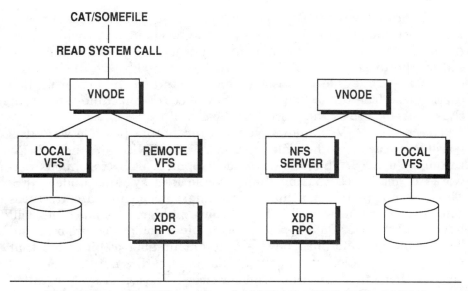

Figure 26. A remote file access under NFS using VFS, RPC and XDR

The NFS has done more than modify the mount command and, effectively, include more mount points for external machines, it has also changed the file system. So as well as allowing the ability to mount in remote file systems, all file accesses are filtered through a virtual file system (VFS). The VFS is the first point of reference for files in the file system, and as well as holding the inode number it also records which file system the file is in and whether it is a local or remote file. If the file is a local one then the file access goes much as one would expect on a normal UNIX system. However if it is remote then a whole sub-system has to be called up to deal with the file access.

In order for NFS to be used the machines must be physically connected and be running the NFS services. The physical connection must be some fast high data rate local area network media such as ethernet as the access time for remotely mounted file systems must be comparable with those of local discs. Unlike the ARPA services, and some of the other networking programs we shall encounter, NFS is achieved by substantial modifications to the UNIX kernel. When the kernel has resolved that a file access is for another machine, a remote procedure call (RPC) is made across the network to that machine to access the file. RPCs are the mechanism by which calls are made to routines that run on another macine. The RPC is processed on the target machine (known as the server), there the requiste checks are made, file permissions and so on, and the action is then carried out. The data is sent back to the source machine (known as the client) for use by the process that called it up.

The use of the VFS allows NFS to operate in a flexibile way. It is possible to access other file systems, both UNIX and non-UNIX, through the VFS. This allows the development of hetrogenuous networks of machines sharing their diverse files systems under NFS. This also means that machines with different machine architectures can inter-communicate. This has obvious problems, as machines will have conflicts over data types; for example a double precission number on one machine may have a different number of bits from that represented on another machine. This requires the network to standardize their data types for transference. NFS uses a system called eXternal Data Representation (XDR). This set of library routines converts all data types between machines into a standard, non-machine specific format for transmission.

As was stated earlier the designers of such systems tried to make the system as transparent as possible to the user. There are some circumstances when this aim is impossible, particularly when the server machine goes down. When this happens the client RPC will be unable to continue its dialogue with its server counterpart, and the user will get messages about NFS servers being unavailable. This will only affect the connection between the client and this particular server, and the machine will be able to go on as normal, so long as it doesn't attempt to access that particular machine. This is because NFS is designed as a stateless network system, where each machine acts both as a client and a server to other machines, but does not maintain a record of its current transactions with any another machine. However in reality file serving machines in NFS networks are so interdependent once one has gone down the other are unable to do any serious work without delays.

A good way to understand NFS is to look at its operation. The command **df** (**d**isk **f**ile systems) on a NFS machine will produce modified output

```
craig@gould1 df
Filesystem    kbytes    used     avail     capacity  Mounted on
/dev/dk0a     23583     17686    3538      83%       /
/dev/dk0d     102607    90552    1794      98%       /usr.PW
/dev/dk1e     95583     38317    47707     45%       /usr.PW
/dev/dk1a     12607     63       11283     1%        /tmp
/dev/dk0f     32911     20165    9454      68%       /sysman
/dev/dk1d     59967     35745    18225     66%       /u1
/dev/dk1f     36095     27073    5412      83%       /u2
/dev/dk0e     78735     59609    11252     84%       /u3
/dev/dk1h     36863     30132    3044      91%       /u4
gould2:/u5    33095     20069    9716      67%       /u5
gould2:/u7    56831     50452    695       99%       /u7
gould2:/u8    47583     25469    17355     59%       /u8
gould2:/ua    37927     1        34133     0%        /ua
gould2:/uc    23439     19672    2595      88%       /uc
gould2:/ub    23783     8376     13028     39%       /ub
gould2:/u9    47583     29223    13601     68%       /u9
sol:/ue       16189     6607     7963      45%       /ue
sol:/uf       16189     6607     7963      45%       /uf
sol:/ug       16189     6607     7963      45%       /ug
sol:/uh       16189     6607     7963      45%       /uh
```

This shows, for remotely mounted file systems, the machine that they are resident on. So if we change directory to **/ue** we are infact accessing files on the remote server **sol**, and any file access will cause a RPC call to be made between the client machine **Gould1** and the server machine **sol**. So doing a command like

craig@gould1 cp /ue/sunfile /ua/gouldfile

is the NFS equivalent of doing a Berkeley ARPA **rcp**

craig@gould1 rcp sol:/ue/sunfile /ua/gouldfile

Obviously the NFS sequence is the easier as no special command is needed nor any knowledge of what machines are being accessed. In terms of NFS's relationship to the ISO 7 layered model it works on all layers from the presentation layer down. Users don't have to initiate sessions, as this is done at system boot-up time, and the presentation problems of their data are taken care of by XDR. NFS is limited though, as its name implies, to file systems served across networks, and does not explicitly provide networked process execution facilities.

111

If the following command is entered, this can also tell us something about a NFS system

```
%26craig@gould1 cd /
%27craig@gould1 ls -i
```

2120 News	6148 lib	6151 u9
13 PCAS	3 lost+found	8199 ua
46 acsload	41 make_test	9 ub
6144 bin	8196 mnt	2056 uc
63 calendar	8202 mnt2	4104 ud
6155 common	19 ranlib.sh	6152 ue
38 datesync	12 src	2057 uh
43 dead.letter	15 sys	16 unix
4096 dev	2059 sysman	36 unix.LAST
8192 etc	6 tmp	18 usr
10 home	8198 u3	2048 usr.POWERNODE
65 junk	8 u5	17 vmunix

If we now remotely login to another UNIX host and do the same set of commands we will see some of the same files, shared via NFS, but they are now imported into another machine's file system so they have different inode numbers, even though they are the same directories.

```
%29craig@ gould1 rlogin zugzwang
```
It will be advantageous to cross the great stream ... the Dragon is on the wing in the Sky ... the Great Man rouses himself to his Work.

```
%%27craig@zugzwang cd /
%%28craig@zugzwang ls -i
```

120 bin	17338 home	122 sys
1259 u5	18043 ue	7013 common
128 kadb	28819 tmp	7010 u9
1260 uh	7014 crt	121 lib
18037 u1	7011 ua	11689 usr
7008 cs	18041 ml	41578 u2
18042 ub	34600 var	34609 dev
119 mnt	1258 u3	7012 uc
127 vmunix	11612 etc	5828 sbin
18038 u4	41580 ud	

```
%28craig@zugzwang ~.
```
Closed connection.

112

you will notice that the although the two machines share a large number of mounted directories, they are distinct and different. Some of the files are not shared and cannot be shared; any binary for example will not be portable to any machine as they are machine specific files. The commands give above, before the **rlogin**, are using the host **gould1**'s kernel to access files, some perhaps via RPC calls over the ethernet, after the **rlogin** command we are using the machine **zugzwang's** kernel.

The nature of shareable and non-portable files can perhaps be illustrated in the following interaction. If we are logged onto one of the our SUN4 hosts, **sol**, and look at a simple 'hello world' C program,

```
%26craig@sol cat world.c
#include <stdio.h>
void main()
  {
  printf("Hello World\n");
  }
```

We can then compile it on the SUN4 using the **cc** command, invoking the C compiler, leaving the binary in the file **world**

```
%27craig@sol cc -o world world.c
```

We can then run the binary by typing in its name at the prompt

```
%28craig@sol world
Hello World
```

getting the expected output. If we then remotely login to another machine,

```
%29craig@sol rlogin g1
Just once, I wish we would encounter an alien menace
that wasn't immune to bullets.
-- The Brigader [Dr. Who]

%26craig@gould1
```

and try to run the same binary

```
%27craig@gould1 world
    world: ***: not found
    world: &(T^Bb@@@@@£@££@££#
    @%%@!!!c?h/$.#b(£@£@£@K: not found
    world: B1: not found
    world: dB#: not found
    world: %%h@: not found
    world: %G: not found
    world: @@c?: not found
    world: §§c?: not found
    world: %1r@: cannot open
    world: @1&@: cannot open
```

We get a whole list of error messages. This is because the compiler created, when executed on the SUN4, a binary to run on that architecture, and when we logged across to the Gould and tried to run it, the **csh** couldn't recognise it as a binary, and tried to interpret it as a **sh** script file! As NFS is only a networked file system and not a distributed processing system, it is not designed to deal with networked process execution problems.

PC-NFS

If you have access to IBM PCs that have ethernet cards and can connect into your UNIX NFS network it is possible that they may be running PC-NFS. PC-NFS is a stripped down implementation of NFS for PCs. It differs from normal NFS in that the PC can only be served by other, normal NFS machines, but it cannot serve them. This means that effectively you have access to UNIX file systems from the PC but you cannot access, using NFS, the PC from UNIX. Also the implementation of NFS suffers limitations concerning file names that are imposed by MSDOS.

However, these caveats aside, PC-NFS is a very useful product that makes file transfer/sharing between PCs and UNIX very easy. Once you have found a PC that is connected to your ethernet, and is running PC-NFS, the first thing to do is to find out what username it has had allocated using the **net name** command.

C:\\>net name
The name of this system is betelgeuse, and its IP address is 192.35.172.12 It is in Yellow Pages domain milkyway, served by sol (192.35.172.1). The authentication server is sol (192.35.172.1). Non-local routing via gateway gould1 (192.35.172.14) You are logged in as nobody, with UID -2 and GID -2.
It is Sun Jun 02 14:31:48 1991, WDT

The system normally defaults to a low privileged user called nobody. The first thing you should do is register your user name with PC-NFS using

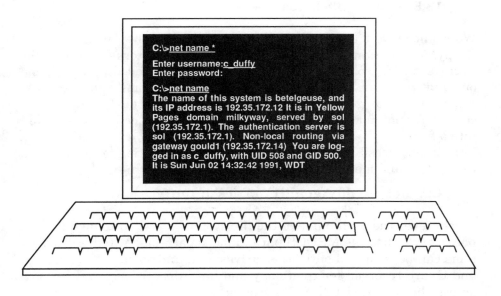

You will see that the output from the **net name** command now shows the newly installed name. PC-NFS has implementations of commands such as **rsh** and **rcp**. If we wished to run some commands on the UNIX file system we could use **rsh**, as in the following

%**rsh sol ls -l**

Which would give a long listing of our home directory on the machine **sol**. Unlike the Berkeley ARPA **rsh** the PC-NFS version does not default to **rlogin** when no command is specified.

115

If we changed our current working directory to the floppy drive A: and then typed in the command

```
C:\>A:
A:\>rcp sol:.emacs cd2.txt

A:\>dir /w
```

Volume in drive A has no label
Directory of A:

TMP	DOS	NFS	NIC	LOGIN
PATH	00IND~PA	DEAD~~QA	PCWRITE	PDSOFT
MARKS	CD TXT	UTILS	RCP TXT	F-PROT

18 File(s)   7708 bytes free

We would have transferred a file from the UNIX system to the PC's floppy. MSDOS and UNIX treat end of line characters differently for Ascii text files, so when transferred files are viewed they may come out a bit peculiar. PC-NFS provides 2 utilities (actually shell scripts) dos2unix and unix2dos. These programs simply output the file in the correct format for each system, and their output can be redirected into a file.

It is also possible to mount in some UNIX partitions into the PC's file system and make them available to MSDOS. Using

```
C:\>net use d: \\gould1\u3\lcs\c_duffy
```

or whatever the path name of the file system you wish to mount. It is necessary to use the MSDOS path name separators, \. Other file systems can be mounted onto other drives; e: f: and so on – drives A:, B: and C: are reserved for the floppy and hard disk drives. We can now access the mounted UNIX file system as though it were an MSDOS device. So doing

```
C:>cp d:\.login a:\login.txt
```

would copy the file from the UNIX system onto the MSDOS formatted floppy in drive A:. Obviously doing the command

```
C:>cp a:\autoexec.bat d:\autoexec.bat
```

Will copy a file from the MSDOS system to the UNIX one. The **mv** command has also been implemented on PC-NFS.

Commands such as the UNIX **ls** and the MSDOS **dir** both work. As MSDOS has a fixed format for file names, it is likely that when they are copied across that the name will have to be truncated. The **dir** command shows the truncated form, whilst the **ls** command shows both the truncated and the UNIX format.

```
C:\>ls d:\doc\
.              <DIR>    11-13-90   3:28p   U:rwx
..             <DIR>    6-02-91    2:35p   U:rwx
BOOK           <DIR>    10-18-90   5:52p   U:rwx
OUTLI~7J       1578     3-14-86    3:30p   U:rw-   outline86-87
TEST   SH      114      3-14-86    3:44p   U:rwx
OUTLI~8B       244      3-12-87    10:19a  U:rw-   outline87-88
ATARI DOC      1413     5-05-88    7:56p   U:rw-
DCO            33416    2-28-86    7:25p   U:rw-
NET_LIST       202      11-23-89   1:57p   U:rw-
MANUAL         24871    6-27-90    5:54p   U:rw-
MAKE           23641    11-13-90   3:28p   U:rw-
```

Once you have finished using the the PC you can use the command

> %**net logout**

or just

> %**logout**

The later will simply call **net logout**, this removes your name from the PC and returns the name to the default nobody. However it does not unmount your file system(s). This is no big problem as nobody has very few priviledges and probably won't be able to change things. However normal paranoia suggests that it is wisest to turn the machine off after use!

Network Information Services

As each machine on a NFS network is a stand-alone version of UNIX with its own kernel, it also has its own **passwd** file. This means that on a network of 20 or 30 workstations, it would be necessary for a user to change their password on all of these individual machines, each time they needed to change their password. This would obviously be an irksome task. To obviate this SUN have supplied a distributed database system, Network Information Services, formerly called Yellow Pages, to centralise and automate this system.

NIS works with a centralised database of the information held in **/etc/passwd**. This central copy denotes a NIS domain, and other machines in this domain will act as servers for password information. This is to stop a bottleneck occurring by password accesses being directed at one machine. When a user wishes to change a password, rather than simply access password information, the server is contacted, its database changed, and then the updated password files pushed across the network for the NIS servers. This can all take some time, as it is subject to delay when machines have difficulty contacting each other. Changing a password with NIS is done by

%**yppasswd**

The system will prompt and respond in much the same way as the **passwd** command does.

Each machine still has it old **/etc/passwd** file, and it is possible to have that used in preference to the NIS version. However in general all password information will be held through NIS. This means that **/etc/passwd** is no longer a good guide to users on the system. There are a series of commands, all preceded with the characters **yp**, from the halcyon days when it was called Yellow Pages, which manipulate the NIS databases. To find a username type:

%**ypmatch r_willia passwd**

This means find the key **r_willia** in the passwd database. It is possible to find information about other password fields or other NIS databases, such as the groups file. To do the equivalent of **cat /etc/passwd** use

%**ypcat passwd**

This will probably list a large amount of information.

Interconnections with Non UNIX Machines

Using FTP

So far we have been concentrating on file transfer and network communications between machines that all run UNIX. It is often necessary to communicate with machines that run different and incompatible operating systems. The file transfer programs that I will describe in the following sections are generally used to transfer files between such machines, although they can be used to transfer between machines running UNIX. In my experience machines that are running UNIX have much easier ways, described in the previous section, to transfer data, so I shall concentrate on file transfer between UNIX and non UNIX machines.

The **ftp** file transfer program requires similar ground rules to the Berkeley ARPA services, in that it requires some form of physical connection and the ability to run the application on both machines. The physical connection must be a fast large bandwidth medium such as ethernet. The ethernet system is described by its formal name, CSMA/CD. As ethernet is a broadcast bus network it allows all stations to monitor, to have Carrier Sense, of all of the network traffic – including the station's own. Having Multiple Access means that all stations can directly access the network. As all stations have multiple access then there is the possibility of contention, that data could collide on the network. Therefore the system needs a mechanism for Collision Detection. The medium access control, data link layer in the ISO model, is handled by the firmware in the ethernet card. As it is a broadcast network there is little routing for the network layer to do. This all means that ethernet allows software such as the Berkeley ARPA, NFS and **ftp** to offer fast concurrent services. There are other local area networks, such as token rings that offer the same functionality, over which **ftp** can operate.

119

ftp is invoked by typing

> %**ftp p2**
> **Connected to prime2.**
>
> **220 Prime FTP Server.**

this will attempt to initiate an **ftp** session with the machine **p2**. If the machine **p2** supports **ftp** then a deamon running on it should pick up the **ftp** connection and initiate the session. The names of remote machines are in a file in **/etc/hosts**. This looks like this

> %**cat /etc/hosts**
>
> | | |
> |---|---|
> | 127.1 | localhost |
> | # | |
> | # Add your systems below – do not change or remove localhost definition above | |
> | # | |
> | #1.2 | sysname SYSNAME Sysname |
> | 192.35.172.1 | sol Sol SOL |
> | 192.35.172.2 | sirius Sirius SIRIUS |
> | 192.35.172.3 | canopus Canopus CANOPUS |
> | 192.35.172.4 | centauri Centauri CENTAURI |
> | 192.35.172.5 | vega Vega VEGA |
> | 192.35.172.6 | capella Capella CAPELLA |
> | 192.35.172.7 | arcturus Arcturus ARCTURUS |
> | 192.35.172.8 | rigel Rigel RIGEL |
> | 192.35.172.9 | procyon Procyon PROCYON |
> | 192.35.172.10 | achernar Achernar ACHERNAR |
> | 192.35.172.11 | altair Altair ALTAIR |
> | 192.35.172.12 | betelgeuse Betelgeuse BETELGEUSE |
> | 192.35.172.13 | wd Wd WD |
> | 192.35.172.14 | gould1 Gould1 GOULD1 g1 G1 |
> | 192.35.172.15 | gould2 Gould2 GOULD2 g2 G2 |
> | 192.35.172.16 | darkstar |
> | 192.35.172.18 | baldric |
> | 192.35.172.40 | ZEUS zeus OLYMPUS olympus   cvax |
> | +: | |

This shows the names, in various formats, of the hosts and their internet addresses. This internet address is a unique address of each machine, or rather for each network connection a machine has. Internet addresses are assigned by a central body, the Networking Information Centre in the United States. They give each machine a unique address within the world-wide Internet network of computers. It is possible to connect to a machine using its internet address, using

%ftp 192.35.172.5

would connect with the machine **vega**. If you have problems getting a response from a machine it is possible to see whether or not it is still on the network by using the **ping** command.

% /usr/etc/ping p2
baldric is alive

All this really tells you is that the ethernet card is functioning and the machine is switched on! You may find that **ping** is not in your search path or in the directory given above, in which case use the **whereis** command to find it. As long as the machine is functioning and the name is correctly given, **ftp** should respond with its prompt

ftp>

It is then possible to connect with the remote machine. If you have specified a machine when calling up **ftp** then it will automatically prompt for a username and password. This will prompt

Name (p2:c_duffy):
331 Enter PASS Command.
Password:
230 User Logged in.

Once you have verified the username and typed in your password you will be able to transfer files. If you do not specify a machine name when calling up **ftp** then it will be necessary to issue **open**, **user** and **pass** commands manually; these command open a connection, login in a user and verify the user's password. Most versions of **ftp** have a simple on-line help which will look something like this.

ftp> <u>help</u>
Commands may be abbreviated. Commands are:

!	cr	macdef	proxy	sendport
$	delete	mdelete	put	status
account	debug	mdir	pwd	struct
append	dir	mget	quit	sunique
ascii	disconnect	mkdir	quote	tenex
bell	form	mls	recv	trace
binary	get	mode	remotehelp	type
bye	glob	mput	rename	user
case	hash	nmap	reset	verbose
cd	help	ntrans	rmdir	?
cdup	lcd	open	runique	
close	ls	prompt	send	

for slightly more detailed help use the format

ftp> <u>help close</u>

will give

close   terminate   ftp   session

The two most used **ftp** commands reflect its main purpose; **get** and **put**, to allow the transmission and reception of files. The syntax is straight forward

ftp> <u>get virus</u>
200 Host 192.35.172.1, port 1177.
150 Retrieval of "virus" started okay.
226 File transfer completed okay.
local: virus remote: virus
14840 bytes received in 0.56 seconds (26 Kbytes/s)

and

ftp> <u>put antidote</u>
200 Host 192.35.172.31, port 1058.
125 Storing "antidote" started okay.
226 File transfer completed okay.
local: antidote remote: antidote
575 bytes sent in 0.1 seconds (5.6 Kbytes/s)

it is possible to change directory on the remote and local machines using the **cd** and **lcd** commands. So

> **ftp>**<u>**lcd thisdir**</u>

would change the local directory to thisdir and

> **ftp>**<u>**cd thatdir**</u>

would change the remote to thatdir.

It is possible to access either single shell command with

> **ftp>**<u>**!date**</u>

or to run a shell from **ftp** with

> **ftp>**<u>**!**</u>
> %

Exiting the shell will return control to **ftp**. **Ftp** can be exited using the **quit** command, or if a further connection is required the current connection can be closed and a new one invoked;

> **ftp>** <u>**quit**</u>
> **221 Disconnect received, closing connections.**
> %

or

> **ftp>**<u>**close**</u>
> **221 Disconnect received, closing connections.**
> **ftp>**<u>**open cvax**</u>
> **Connected to zeus.**
> **220 ZEUS FTP server ready.**
> **Name (cvax:c_duffy):**
> **331 Password required for C_DUFFY.**
> **Password:**
> **230 User C_DUFFY logged in.**

FTP under PC-NFS

The PC-NFS package contains a version of **ftp** within it. It works almost in exactly the same way as the **ftp** outlined above. It is a good idea to register your name with PC-NFS using the **net name** * command, otherwise **ftp** will default to the user name nobody. Once running **ftp** operates exactly as described above, including the help system, apart from the shell escape. Typing **!** will run a new version of command.com, the MSDOS shell,

>ftp>!

>>AKHTER-DOS Version 3.30 (R3)
>>(C)Copyright Microsoft Corp 1981–1987

>C:\>exit

To get back to **ftp** type in **exit**. PC-NFS also includes a program called telnet which works in the same fashion on PCs and minis.

A footnote on Telnet

Telnet is a command that allows terminal/user connection, it works over the ethernet, so allows multiple connections. Unlike **rlogin** it runs on non UNIX machines, so allows terminal connections to machines that run **ftp**. It is invoked in the same way as **ftp**

>%telnet g1

or using an internet number

>%telnet 192.35.172.14

You will then get some sort of message from the remote terminal server

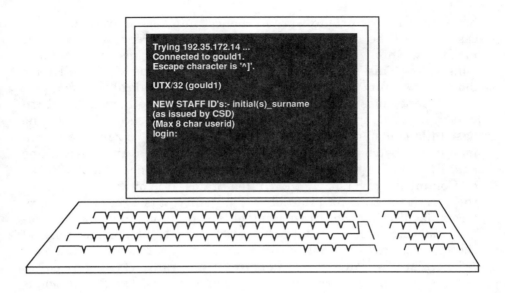

```
Trying 192.35.172.14 ...
Connected to gould1.
Escape character is '^]'.

UTX/32 (gould1)

NEW STAFF ID's:- initial(s)_surname
(as issued by CSD)
(Max 8 char userid)
login:
```

It is then possible to login as you normally would. There are a series of escape commands within **telnet**, all preceded by **^]** . These allow the user to drop back to **telnet** level. For example using

> %**^]**
> **telnet>**

allows the user to drop back to the remote **telnet**, this could then allow the user to issue shell commands on their local machine or even connect to another remote!

Logging off from a connection will terminate the **telnet** session, as will typing

> **^]**
> **telnet> quit**
> **Connection closed.**

Slower fIle transfer programs

So far we have been describing network and file transfer communications that run over ethernet or some other fast larger bandwidth local area networks. It is possible that some of your machines will neither

125

have the software or hardware to connect into such a system. In this case you will be using serial cables, pieces of wire, to connect your machines. This will have a slower data rate and has much smaller bandwidth. This means that the software running on it will have more limited functionality and be slower. The standard interfaces for serial connections are RS232C/V.24. Whereas the ethernet based **ftp** will operate at approximately 100,000 bytes per second, serial line based file transfer programs are much more likely to run at approximately 100 bytes per second. The most ubiquitous of these serial line based ftps is the **kermit** file transfer program, which was developed by Columbia University in the United States. It is often referred to as the kermit file transfer protocol, for, in reality, it is a set of rules (protocols) facilitating the transferring of files from one machine to another and the programs that we use are merely implementations of these rules. **kermit** seems to run on every type of machine available.

There are two ways to use **kermit** for file transfer; using a dedicated line or one that is also used for terminal access. The first option is normally used when transferring between minicomputers (or mainframes). The second, more common application, is usually for microcomputer to minicomputer transfers. See figure 27 and 28.

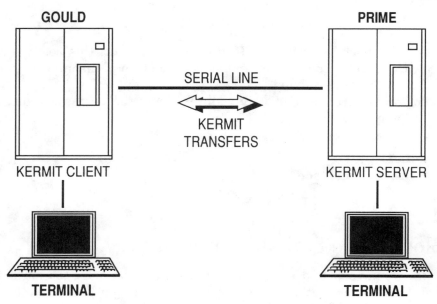

*Figure 27. a **kermit** connection between 2 minis*

126

Although these two modes differ in detail they essentially work in the same way. To transfer the files from one machine to another it is necessary to be able to run a version of **kermit** on both machines. **Kermit** works in a client-server mode; that is, one of the **kermit** programs issues commands and the other **kermit** attempts to service those commands. Once the two programs are running and have established a client-server relationship it is possible for file transfer requests to be issued. In order for these to be successful both **kermit**s must agree certain communications parameters. The other, rather obvious, requirement is that the two machines are connected physically. For the details of the device name of this connection contact your system administrator.

Minicomputer to Minicomputer transfers

In this rather common scenario one has data on another mini or mainframe computer, one not running UNIX, but it is necessary to collect together all the files onto one UNIX machine. In order to complete this file transfer it is necessary to have accounts on both machines, and to be able to run **kermit** on both of them. It is possible to do the transfer from either end; namely to login to the non UNIX machine and send the data across to UNIX or to login to the UNIX machine and get the data from the other machine. In the following dialogue we are assuming that the user is logged into the UNIX host and has an account on the remote machine.

To run **kermit** type in

%**kermit**

kermit will probably give you some information and then respond with its own prompt

C-kermit>

Some versions of **kermit** will have on-line help, on the Bristol Poly UNIX system typing **help** or **?** will get

C-Kermit>? Command, one of the following:

!	bye	close	connect
cwd	dial	directory	echo
exit	finish	get	help
log	quit	receive	remote
script	send	server	set
show	space	statistics	take

Further help can be gained by

C-Kermit>help connect
Connect to a remote system via the tty device given in the most recent 'set line' command

You will find that in this, as in many other areas, **kermit**s are not very standardised.

In order to connect to your remote machine you will need to set the line so that **kermit** works with the dedicated line. Some systems will be set up to do this automatically: therefore you will need to check what line you are using by typing the **show** command

C-kermit>show

this will result in something like this

Communications Parameters:
Line: /dev/tty, speed: -1, mode: remote, modem-dialer: direct
Parity: none, duplex: full, flow: xon/xoff, handshake: none

Protocol Parameters:	Send	Receive
Timeout:	10	7
Padding:	0	0
Pad Character:	0	0
Packet Start:	1	1
Packet End:	13	13
Packet Length:	90	90

Block Check Type: 1, Delay: 5

File parameters:

File Names: converted	Debugging Log: none
File Type: text	Packet Log: none
File Warning: off	Session Log: none
File Display: on	Transaction Log: none

Incomplete File Disposition: discard, Init file: .kermrc

if line is set to local or /dev/tty then it will be necessary to change the line setting using the **set** command

C-kermit>set line /dev/tty29

Once your are connected to the correct line you then need to login to the remote system using the **connect** command

C-kermit>connect

This will then allow you to login to the system you wish to get files from by facilitating a direct connection to the remote machine through the dedicated serial line. At this point you should get a message from **kermit** telling you how to drop back to the local **kermit**. This key sequence should be remembered as it will come in very useful later on. The dialogue I will show you is connecting to the Bristol Poly VAX/VMS system.

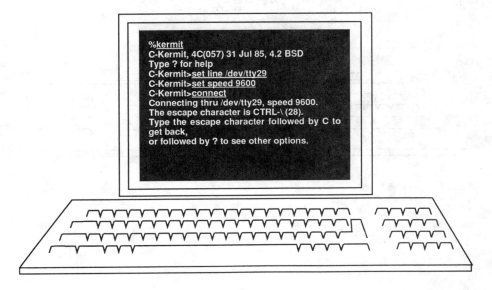

```
%kermit
C-Kermit, 4C(057) 31 Jul 85, 4.2 BSD
Type ? for help
C-Kermit>set line /dev/tty29
C-Kermit>set speed 9600
C-Kermit>connect
Connecting thru /dev/tty29, speed 9600.
The escape character is CTRL-\ (28).
Type the escape character followed by C to
get back,
or followed by ? to see other options.
```

This will then give you your standard login sequence for your machine. It is worth remembering the escape sequence, given above (**^\c**), as you will need it when you wish to drop back from **kermit** to your remote host.

> **Type "C system <RET>". For a list of systems type "H <RET>".**
>
> **Command: c cvax**
> **Break-in : BREAK Abort Output : NONE Interrupt**
> **Process : NONE**
> **Trying to make connection...**
> **[Open]**

On the Bristol system, **kermit** connects through to a terminal server, which facilitates connections to a number of machines. Once through the terminal server the normal login sequence should be followed.

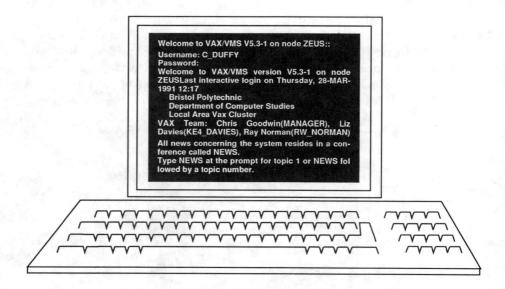

Welcome to VAX/VMS V5.3-1 on node ZEUS::
Username: C_DUFFY
Password:
Welcome to VAX/VMS version V5.3-1 on node ZEUSLast interactive login on Thursday, 28-MAR-1991 12:17
    Bristol Polytechnic
    Department of Computer Studies
    Local Area Vax Cluster
VAX Team: Chris Goodwin(MANAGER), Liz Davies(KE4_DAVIES), Ray Norman(RW_NORMAN)
All news concerning the system resides in a conference called NEWS.
Type NEWS at the prompt for topic 1 or NEWS followed by a topic number.

Once on the remote machine change to the directory holding your data or where you wish the data to be placed. Then run **kermit** on the remote machine,

> **vax <u>kermit</u>**
> **VMS Kermit-32 version 3.1.066**
> **Default terminal for transfers is: _LTA883:**

It will then be necessary to make sure that the remote **kermit** is also talking to the same line, using the vax **kermit** commands

> **Kermit-32> <u>show all</u>**

if the line is not set correctly then it will need setting up

> **Kermit-32> <u>set line LTA883:</u>**

Obviously these setting, and sometimes the format of the commands will vary dependent upon which machine you connect to and which version of **kermit** you execute. Now put the remote **kermit** into server mode

> **Kermit-32> <u>server</u>**
> **Kermit Server running on VAX/VMS host. Please type your escape sequence to return to your local machine. Shut down the server by typing the Kermit BYE command on your local machine.**

At this point the terminal will appear to lock up – as the remote **kermit** is now waiting for message packets from the other **kermit** in order to allow them to transfer files. This is when you need to be able to remember the escape sequence to allow you to drop back to your local kermit. On the Bristol UNIX **kermit** it is ^\, followed by a command, using ^\? gives us a help menu from the host **kermit**

> **C to close the connection, or:**
> **0   (zero) to send a null**
> **B   to send a BREAK**
> **H   to hangup and close connection**
> **S   for status**
> **?   for help**
> **escape character twice to send the escape character.**

Command>c

[Back at Local System]
C-Kermit>

Once having issued the escape sequence the local **kermit** prompt should be back and you can now either **get** the data from the remote machine

> **C-kermit> get bulk.txt**
> **IRN%T%N%N%N%SS%F**
> **BULK.TXT => bulk.txt**
> **CTRL-F to cancel file, CTRL-R to resend current packet**
> **CTRL-B to cancel batch,CTRL-A for status report: %%.%..**
> **^A Status report:**
> **file type: text**
> **file number: 1**
> **characters : 1097**
> **block check: 1**
> **compression: 1**
> **8th-bit prefixing: 1**
> **%..%Z [OK]**

or send files to the remote machine using the **put** command. The Bristol UNIX **kermit** is reasonably user friendly, namely it gives some messages (all of the IRN% messages!) and information to the users, many **kermits** are taciturn creatures.

Don't be too surprised if the transfer takes some time - large files can be quite slow to transfer – some versions of **kermit**, like the one above, give status information while they are getting and putting. If the transaction hangs up, don't worry about it as **kermit** will eventually time out. Problems with transfers causing time outs can be due to a variety of factors. The line may be very noisy and will have continual errors forcing **kermit** to retransmit a large number of times or a more likely reason is that there is an incompatibility between the local and remote **kermits**' transfer and communication settings. These incompatibilities can vary from: the type of data transferred, it can be a text or binary file; there can be differences in the size of packet that **kermit** uses to send data out over the network, this is normally a default size of 90 characters; or the format of the data bytes, 8 bits no parity, one stop bit and so on. With the preceding parameters your local **kermit** guru will be able to tell you which parameters should be set and to what. To alter the default settings simply do a **show** command on both machines and compare the parameters and make the two **kermits** compatible using the **set** command.

Assuming the transmissions all go well eventually then the remote server should be terminated. This can be achieved by one of two commands, **finish** and **bye**. **Finish** stops the remote **kermit** being a server but leaves the dedicated line logged in and the remote **kermit** running in normal mode. **Bye** terminates the server, **kermit** and logs out from the dedicated line. Unless the remote **kermit** is released from server mode the line will be unavailable for some time – a regular source of frustration for other users.

We can see by relating **kermit** back to our ISO model that it only operates on the bottom four layers. Unlike ARPA or **ftp**, it is necessary to do the session creation manually, namely to login to the remote and run **kermit** yourself.

Micro to mini/mainframe transfers

The transfers we have dealt with so far have been those between machines with the ability to have ports dedicated to file transfer. Figure 27 shows this relationship. With microcomputers the transaction is somewhat different, as the line used to login a terminal to the larger machine is the same line used for file transfer – see Figure 28.

In order to do this type of file transfer it is necessary to have both a terminal emulator package, similar to **telnet**, and a version of **kermit** for your micro. The terminal emulator, there are lots of them around, simply makes your micro act like a terminal to allow you to login to a larger machine. On many machines the terminal emulator and **kermit** are built in to the same package, so switching from one to the other is easier. In order to use the terminal emulator to login to UNIX it is also necessary to have a physical connection to the UNIX machine – this is exactly the same type of connection that a normal terminal uses – a serial line connected through a /dev/tty port.

As long as you have all these things a file transfer between the micro and a UNIX machine is possible. In the following description I

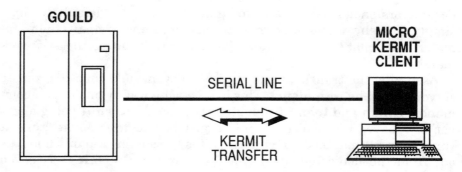

GOULD

MICRO
KERMIT
CLIENT

SERIAL LINE

KERMIT
TRANSFER

*Figure 28. Micro to mini **kermit** transfer*

shall illustrate the dialogue by showing a transfer between an Apple Macintosh and UNIX. Running **kermit** on the Mac allows a connection to the UNIX system, permitting a login as one normally would through a terminal.

```
 File  Settings  Remote  Transfer
▤□▤▤▤▤▤▤▤▤▤▤▤▤ MacKermit ▤▤▤▤▤▤▤▤▤▤▤▤▤
(Max 8 char userid)
login: c_duffy
Password:
Honorable: Afflicted with an impediment in one's reach.  In legislative
bodies, it is customary to mention all members as honorable; as, "the
honorable gentleman is a scurvy cur."
            -- Ambrose Bierce, "The Devil's Dictionary"

%26craig @ gould1 kermit
C-Kermit, 4C(057) 31 Jul 85, 4.2 BSD
Type ? for help
/dev/tty29: 9600 baud
C-Kermit>set line
C-Kermit>seet
?Invalid - seet
C-Kermit>set parity none
C-Kermit>server

C-Kermit server starting.  Return to your local machine by typing
its escape sequence for closing the connection, and issue further
commands from there.  To shut down the C-Kermit server, issue the
FINISH or BYE command and then reconnect.

# N3
```

*Figure 29. An example of logging in through the Macintosh **kermit** screen. The menu bar at the top gives access to **kermit** commands.*

134

Once logged in change to the directory you wish to transfer files into or out of. Then run **kermit** on the UNIX machine and at the prompt put it into server mode (see previous section). Before putting it into server mode it is worth making sure that the line is set to the local tty line and not some other, directly connected, tty port. To find out is this is the case use the **show** command, and verify that line is set to local. If it is not then use the **set** command

C-kermit>set line tty

We now need to return to the micro and issue **kermit** commands. If we are running an integrated terminal emulator/**kermit** then we simply need to type in the required key sequence, for example with the Procom terminal emulator / file transfer package on the IBM PC it is ^k. With our Mac example we simply use the mouse pointer to access the correct pull down menu. If we are running separate terminal emulator and **kermit** programs we will need to return control back to the microcomputer operating system. This is can be achieved by pressing a key sequence which will abort the terminal emulation program; eg on the Atari 1040 pressing the **undo** key.

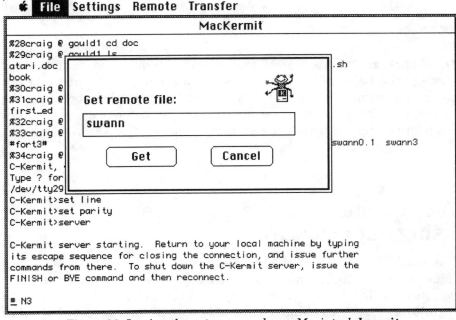

*Figure 30. Issuing the **get** command on a Macintosh **kermit***

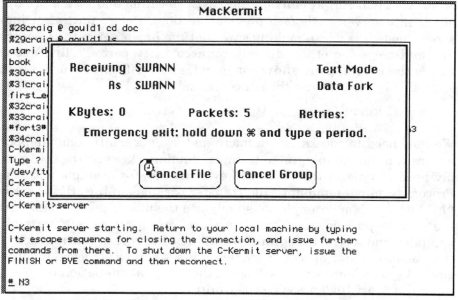

*Figure 31. Status information whilst using **get** on the Macintosh **kermit***

Once back to the control of the micro's operating system **kermit** should then be executed – this allows the the use of the **put** and **get** commands giving the user the ability to transfer data between the machines. The session is terminated in the same ways as earlier transfers using the **finish** or **bye** commands.

A crude method of file transfer using data capture

The method I am about to describe is very crude and unwieldy, but under certain, fairly uncommon, circumstances it may be the only way to transfer data. Put simply it requires the user to able to both login to a remote machine and be able to maintain a record of all of the computer's interactions. This will allow the user to login to the remote machine, the one holding the data to be transferred, from the local machine, the machine the user wishes the data to be transferred to. Once the user has logged across from the local to the remote machine, then it simply requires the listing to the screen of the data to be transferred. This method obviously requires that there is a direct serial link connecting the UNIX machine and the other machine. This link is merely a serial cable coming from one of the /dev/tty ports, which are normally used for terminal access, that has been directly connected to terminal port of another machine. To find out if this has already been done, or is possible, you would have contact your system administrator, who would also have had to have changed the system set up to stop UNIX treating that line as a normal terminal/login port.

Armed with the knowledge of which port is directly connected to our remote machine we now need a command to allow us to login to that machine and a command to maintain a record of our session. The latter command is called **script**, and is evoked by typing

> %**script**
> **Script started on Wed Mar 27 17:07:24 1991**

This will then maintain a record, in a file called **typescript**, of the session that follows. This will include all of the commands typed in by the user and all of the responses made by UNIX. So if we followed the above command by

> %**ls**
> **inferno paradise purgatory**
> %**cat paradise**
> **The glory of Him who moves all things soe'er**
> **Impenetrates the universe, and bright**
> **The splendour burns, more here and less there.**

all of the data would be captured. To complete the data capture type **^d** at the prompt sign and that will end that session – be careful as pressing **^d** more than once may log you out! The record of the session will have been saved in the file called **typescript** which is a normal ASCII text file. It is possible to ask script to place the record in a named file using the command line

> %**script cantica3**

thus placing the record in the file **cantica3**. Using the argument **-a** the session can be appended to the contents of a file.

> %**script -a divine.comedy**

Will append the session following onto the file **divine.comedy**.

The other requirement for file transfer is a program to allow users to login to another machine. There are two versions of this program, one is called **tip**, on Berkeley UNIX, the other **cu** (Call UNIX) on System V. I shall describe the **cu** command and show where **tip** differs from it.

Now it may be that the machine you wish to talk to is a really remote machine and will require modems to allow the communication over the telephone system. If this is the case then the system will have to be set up with files in **/L.sys** for **cu** or **/etc/remote** for **tip.** These files will contain all the information necessary to make the connection – telephones numbers, line speeds, character size and so on. All you would need to know is the name of the machine. If the machine was called florence then you would type

> %**cu florence**

cu would then wait for a while whilst it tries to make the connection. It will then respond with

> **Connected**

Followed by whatever the login prompt is on the machine you wish to connect to. What is more likely to be the case though, is that you are told the port number of the direct line to your 'local' remote machine. In this instance you would type

> % **cu -l /dev/tty29**
> **Connected**

Assuming that the direct line is the port **/dev/tty29**. This should then give you the login prompt. At this prompt you should login and the system will seem and act just like a normal login session. So on the Bristol Polytechnic Prime System we would get

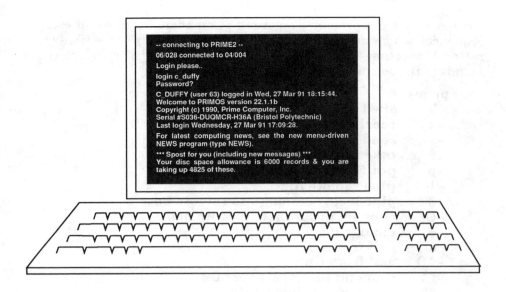

```
-- connecting to PRIME2 --
06/028 connected to 04/004
Login please..
login c_duffy
Password?
C_DUFFY (user 63) logged in Wed, 27 Mar 91 18:15:44.
Welcome to PRIMOS version 22.1.1b
Copyright (c) 1990, Prime Computer, Inc.
Serial #S036-DUQMCR-H36A (Bristol Polytechnic)
Last login Wednesday, 27 Mar 91 17:09:28.
For latest computing news, see the new menu-driven
NEWS program (type NEWS).
*** Spost for you (including new messages) ***
Your disc space allowance is 6000 records & you are
taking up 4825 of these.
```

Once logged into PRIME it is then possible to issue normal PRIMOS (Prime's Operating System) commands as one would if one had logged in in the normal way. Issuing the **ld** (List Directory) command for example, would be captured in our script.

prime ld

<USERL>CS>C_DUFFY (ALL access)
414 records in this directory, 4825 total records out of quota of 6000.

124 Files.

.LOGIN	.POST	A.OUT.H	ASS.2	B.OUT.H
BASTUT.2	BS.TST	C_ALP_88	C_ALP_90	C_CPS_88
CC	CC68.C	CD.EXM	CDTXT	CD_TEMP

....

Once you have located the files you wish to transfer simply list them to the screen. So to look at the file **swann** on a prime computer this would be the command line

prime slist swann

Once you have looked at all the files you wish to transfer then you can logout from the remote system. However you will have to end the **cu** session as logging out of the remote system will only drop you back to the remote's login prompt. To get out of **cu** there are a set of escape sequences which **cu** will pick up, all beginning with the ~ tilde character. Using the ~? command it is possible to get a listing of the commands to the screen.

prime ~?

~!	**shell**
~<	**receive file from remote host**
~>	**send file to remote host**
~t	**take file from remote UNIX**
~p	**put file to remote UNIX**
~I	**pipe remote file**
~$	**pipe local command to remote host**
~C	**connect program to remote host**
~c	**change directory**
~.	**exit from tip**
~^D	**exit from tip**
~^Y	**suspend tip (local+remote)**
~^Z	**suspend tip (local only)**
~s	**set variable**
~?	**get this summary**
~#	**send break**

As you will see from the **cu/tip** help menu there is the possibility of doing file transfer, the **p** and **t** options both require the remote to be running UNIX, the < and > should work with other systems. In practice I have found that if both systems are UNIX there are better ways of transferring files, and if they are not both UNIX then < and > tend to be unreliable.

To end the session use ~. (tilde dot) or ~^d (tilde control d). This will result in

~.
[EOT]

As you have been running the script command on the UNIX system you will have a record of everything that was sent to the screen – including the file you wished to transfer! All you need to do is end the script running on your host machine by typing **^d**, and you should have all your data captured.

This method is very crude as everything during the session is recorded and so will require extraneous information removing from the data file – and if you wished to transfer more than one file you would have to enter an editor and split them manually. As this method is only data capture, and not really file transfer, it is very slow as it will only transfer at the rate that data is displayed on the terminal. As it is simply a record of the transaction there is no error detection or correction, so all the transmission errors will be picked up. Only text files can transferred, as it is impossible to list binary files onto a terminal screen. Finally, it also has the jolly useful feature that whilst doing the transfer the terminal is locked up and completely unusable.

Obviously this method is only used under extreme circumstances, either when the software or hardware just isn't available or when it has broken.

LANS, WANS and Network Addressing

Network Addressing

A source of confusion to many UNIX users is the differing and often contradictory means of addressing users and machines over networks. Some of the complexity comes from the history of UNIX, where systems that were built to respond to particular and specific needs have had an impact beyond those origins. Some of it comes from commercial rivalry generating incompatibility.

The simplest way of trying to deal with these problems is to reduce the problem to a simpler one we all understand, that of sending letters via the postal system. We all understand addresses written in this fashion

```
Craig Duffy
Computer Studies Dept
Bristol Polytechnic
Frenchay
Bristol
BS16 1QY
UK
```

And we could still understand it if it were in a different format. For example with commas at the end of each line, or with some of the fields joined together. We even don't feel perturbed by the technical details, BS16 1QY, that is included for the postal services' use. How we understand this, and what we need to understand, depends upon where the letter is from. If we are sending it from within the British Isles, then the UK is redundant, so

```
Craig Duffy
Computer Studies Dept
Bristol Polytechnic
Frenchay
Bristol
BS16 1QY
```

would do. If I were using the internal mail at the Polytechnic, which would be curious as I would be mailing to myself!, I could use

Craig Duffy
Computer Studies Dept

So what we are reading is a set of narrowing approximations leading to a final, specified, recipient. And just how many approximations are needed depends upon the context of the message, from where it is sent. Each area does not need to know any details about another area other than how to get it there. For example the postal workers in France only need to know how to get the letter to the UK but will not need to know anything about Bristol.

Addressing users on computers is fairly similar. Like most things to do with computers, the addresses have to be in a very strict format. Computers do not have friendly postal workers and will not be able to interpret ambiguous addresses. Also computer networks are not standardised, and there are major vendor specific differences. However computer networks offer much more than just a mail service, so over a network it is possible to mail, file transfer (a bit like parcel post!), interactively talk, remotely run jobs and remotely login.

Another feature of computer networking which sometimes confuses users is that one machine may support many different types of networking software and protocols. It may also belong to a number of different networks of computers. So the UNIX machines at Bristol Polytechnic support UUCP (which provides features such as **cu**), the Internet tcp/ip protocols (providing **ftp** and **telnet**), Berkeley ARPA services, NFS, JANET and good old **kermit**! All of these systems will have slight differences, and will provide complementary and often overlapping features.

If you are contacting a user on the same machine as the one you are logged into, then there is no need for addressing, so

%**mail craig**

will do. However when we wish to address a user on another machine, or wish to become a user on another machine, we must then find some way of specifying the machine. There has grown up two differing ways of specifying machine addresses under UNIX. One is known as bang addressing, the other internet or domain addressing.

Bang addressing, so called because it uses the ! (bang) character or exclamation mark to separate machine names, comes from the UUCP system. The UUCP system, UNIX to UNIX Copy Program, was developed in the early 1970s to network UNIX machines using RS232 serial line and modem technology. **cu** was developed as part of UUCP, other programs allowed file copy across machines, mailing to remote machine and remote login facilities. The UUCP network of computers grew up in a piece-meal, co-operative fashion, and is still one of the largest networks of computer users. In order to connect to a machine using UUCP, it was necessary to know what machines your own host and the remote host where connected to. To specify the remote machine was simply to put the remote file/username followed by each machine that had to connected through to separated by a ! character. So we could mail to user **craig** on machine **gould2** via the following pathname

%mail sol!gould2!craig

This has two disadvantages; if your are using a **csh** then you will have to escape each of the ! characters with a backslash character, secondly it is necessary to spell out the entire pathname for the machine.

Internet addressing uses the idea of machine domains. This means that groups of machines are organised into domains and within these there are sub-domains. These are machine hierarchies, which means that you only need to know which domain a machine or user is in, not a list of machines that lead to it. Normally within one domain one would merely have to state the user at a particular host within that domain

%mail craig@gould2

if the message were to pass through multiple domains, then each domain should be listed, separated by a period (.) mark

%mail craig@uk.ac.brispoly.gould2

So reading left to right the uk domain contains the academic (ac) sub-domain which contains the sub-domain Bristol Poly (brispoly) and finally Bristol has a host which is the machine gould2. The above address is given as an address within the **janet** network. **Janet** (joint academic **net**work) is a network of computer users within uk academic institutions. If your institution has got the hardware, software and paid the membership fees it may be possible for you use **janet** for mailing, file transfer and remote login across the uk. You could even try mailing the above address! You may notice when looking at network addresses from Europe and the US that they differ slightly,

mmarak@csi.forth.gr

The difference is in how to read the address, sometimes called the sex of the address. The two styles of addressing are called big-endian and little-endian. The uk uses little-endian. This means that reading, from left-to-right, the general domain to the more particular domains, ending up with the littlest, the target host, on the end. So with the above we go from the United Kingdom domain (uk), to the academic domain (ac) to Bristol Polytechnic (brispoly) ending up at the host gould2. With the other big-endian addresses, used in Europe and the USA, they start with the particular going to the general. So much for international networking standards!

It is possible that your system mail program will be able to cope with **janet** addresses, like the one given above. However it is possible that you will have to use a special program to mail across **janet**. Remotely logging in over **janet** normally requires access to a piece of hardware called a **pad** (packet assembler disassembler). The pad allows connection through the X.25 protocols to the **janet** network. On the Bristol UNIX system only one machine, Gould2, is connected to the pad, so it is necessary to log through to that machine to run a janet session. Once on Gould2 the pad is called up

```
%pad
PAD>
```

It is then possible to connect through to a another machine, so long as you know of a machine where you have a user account. It is possible to connect through to some information server machines on the network which have fairly open access. One is called **janet.news**, to connect use

```
%%26craig @ gould2 pad
PAD> call uk.ac.janet.news
pad: Calling ...
Connected, break-in character is ^p
To enter command state type ^p followed by 'a'
This is the JANET NEWS machine – log in with the id
NEWS
```

Once through to the janet news machine there is a guest user id, called news which has no password, which allows users to login into and use the janet news service.

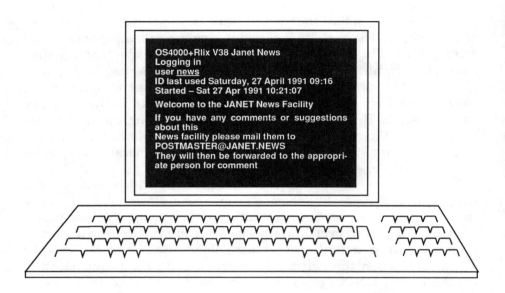

```
OS4000+Rlix V38 Janet News
Logging in
user news
ID last used Saturday, 27 April 1991 09:16
Started – Sat 27 Apr 1991 10:21:07

Welcome to the JANET News Facility

If you have any comments or suggestions
about this
News facility please mail them to
POSTMASTER@JANET.NEWS
They will then be forwarded to the appropri-
ate person for comment
```

Once you have found the information you require, then you either logout of the system or use **^p** to drop back to the pad. Then all that is necessary is to quit from the pad or make another connection.

PAD>_q

Call cleared (00 00) Free   00+00:00:45   6/41

Most pads have a simple help system which is called up by the **?** command, which lists the available commands:

PAD> ?
Commands are (see help for more details): echo, dfwt,
break, crpad, width, speed, lfinsert, edit, erase, kill,
retype, breakin, werase, loghost, message, par, set,
call, clear, status, reset, help, l, q, s, r, p, rcall, i, S,
tcall, file, profile, prompt, commands

And the help command which either gives the menu below or extra information on nominated commands.

146

PAD> help
PAD commands: (further help available using help
<command>)

!command	execute command (in subshell)
break	send X25 Interrupt/TS Expedite
call addr	make an X29 context call
clr	clear call
commands	compact list of all commands available
file	send file upline (as if typed)
i alias	decode alias/entityname; insert result as data
l	report status of X25 link
p	exit from break-in; proceed with call
par	list current PAD parameter set
q	quit pad
r	repeat previous call
rcall addr	repeatedly call
reset	send X25/TS Reset
s file	create file and store received data
S file	Append received data to file (or create)
set	set parameters
stat	print status of current session
tcall addr	make a TS29 context call

Full list: echo, dfwt, break, crpad, width, speed,
lfinsert, edit, erase, kill, retype, breakin, werase,
loghost, message, par, set, call, clear, status, reset,
help, l, q, s, r, p, rcall, i, S, tcall, file, profile, prompt,

There are also machines which act as public domain software servers,
from which it is possible to down-load software from a variety of sour-
ces for a variety of machines. One such machine is the Lancaster
University's **lancs.pdsoft** machine. It is possible to login to this
machine, using

%27craig @ gould2 pad
PAD> call lancs.pdsoft
pad: Calling ...
Connected, break-in character is ^p
To enter command state type ^p followed by 'a'
Lancaster University Computer Centre
(uk.ac.lancs.pdsoft)
Sequent Symmetry S27 / Dynix 3 Network Terminal
Service

Once the machine has been called up then it is possible to login to a guest account, called **pdsoft** using the password **pdsoft**. The system has a UNIX like restricted shell environment which is easy to get round.

> **For access to NPDSA use username "pdsoft" and**
> **password "pdsoft"**
> **login:** <u>pdsoft</u>
> **Password:**
>
> **NPDSA SHELL 2.10.000 started (Users 5/45, Load 2.78)**
>
> **Useful Commands To Get You Started**
> \-
> **?   Lists the commands you can use**
> **help   Enters interactive help system**
> **news   micros or news kermit   Latest news on**
> **   micro or kermit software topics**

The machine is a large store of public domain software which can be down loaded to your local machine. The software covers machines like the Macintosh, Atari, Amiga, IBM PC and BBC, and has a broad range of packages from Bible concordance packages to C compilers. Normally one logs in to get some basic information and then relies upon transferring files using a file transfer protocol.

The ftp used is different from the ftp program outlined earlier. This one, normally called **hhcp** (**h**ost-to-**h**ost **c**o**p**y), uses a protocol, NIFTP (network independent file transfer protocol) that allows file transfers across the janet network. On the lancs.pdsoft machine each directory has a file called **00contents** which is a contents list. So to get the one for the Atari source code we would use

> **%<u>hhcp uk.ac.lancs.pdsoft:micros/atari/00contents</u>**
> **<u>contents</u>**
> **[uk.ac.lancs.pdsoft: no stored attributes]**
> **transfer authorisation:** <u>pdsoft</u>
> **transfer password:**
> **contents: transfer id is 009677**

It is necessary to give a user account and password to **hhcp**, however we already know the details for the **pdsoft** account. It is also possible to transfer files from your local machine to remote machines, simply by change the order of the command parameters. A remote file transfer can take some time, and it is possible to find out how your job is doing using the **hhq** command

```
%hhq
Owner    Id       Address      Status    Size    Files
c_duffy  009678 lancs.pdsoft 1.1.1RP 0 /u3/c_duffy/contents
root     -        -            545.1.5TP 5213   MAIL
root     -        -            482.1.2TP 5213   MAIL
root     -        -            481.1.1TP 5213   MAIL
root     -        -            480.2.0TP 5213   MAIL
```

It is possible to remove jobs from the queue by using the **hhrm** command with the id number given by **hhcp** and **hhq**. If anything goes wrong with the transfer you will normally get a mail message explaining what it, either the remote or local machine, thinks went wrong.

There are some machines on the janet network, and on other networks, that act as information servers. There is one for information about the large American network NSFNET. If you mail it a request, in a prescribed format, then it will send you information about that topic. So to get the general index for the server just mail

```
%mail info-server@uk.ac.nsfnet-relay
Subject: index
request: index
topic: index
request: end
.
EOT
```

To get information on different subject areas just use a different topic name. The machine will automatically mail back the information required, if you make an error with the format of your request, you will get an error message mailed to you! This way of getting information is easier than using **hhcp** as you don't need to known any usernames or passwords. There are many machines offering information services, many of them can be found through janet news.

Finally it is possible that your institution has subscribed to the **uknet** network. This network, also called **usenet** in the US, allows users to subscribe and contribute to notice boards and mail over an international network of machines. There are hundreds of different interest groups, from computing to politics and sport, as well as many more esoteric subjects. Your system manager will be able to tell you if

149

you are on **uknet**, if you are not then you should ask to be! To read the bulletin board use the **trn** command (threaded **r**ead **n**ews). There are hundreds of different news groups, and it is possible to specify in your **.newsrc** file which you wish to read when they are updated. Typing **trn** will produce the following output

> **%26craig@gould2** <u>**trn**</u>
> **(Revising soft pointers--be patient.)**
> | | |
> |---|---|
> | **Unread news in soc.culture.new-zealand** | **58 articles** |
> | **Unread news in sci.geo.meteorology** | **37 articles** |
> | **Unread news in brispoly.test** | **3 articles** |
> | **Unread news in brispoly.mcitalk** | **9 articles** |
> | **Unread news in rec.arts.comics** | **257 articles** |
> | **etc.** | |

Once **trn** has told you about some unread groups, it will then check your **.newsrc** file for against any new groups, and ask you if you wish to add them. When you first start using **uknet** this can be a slow process.

> **Checking active list for new newsgroups...**
>
> **Newsgroup alt.fan.rush-limbaugh not in .newsrc--add? [yn]** <u>**n**</u>
> **Newsgroup comp.sys.hp48 not in .newsrc--add? [yn]**<u>**n**</u>
> **Newsgroup comp.sys.hp48.d not in .newsrc--add? [yn]** <u>**n**</u>
> **Newsgroup comp.org.acm not in .newsrc--add? [yn]** <u>**y**</u>
> **Put newsgroup where? [$^.L]** <u>**CR**</u>
> **Newsgroup rec.music.christian not in .newsrc--add? [yn]** <u>**n**</u>

After that you will be prompted to read the new information in each news group

> ********58 unread articles in soc.culture.new-zealand**
> **--read**
> **now? [+ynq]**

So that you can either read it or skip onto the next news group. **trn** is not one of the easiest of commands to use. If your system has the gnu emacs editor then a much better option is the gnus command.

User to User Communication

The simplest form of communication is to use the **write** command to write directly to a user. The **who** command can be used to find out who is logged onto the system, as you can only write to logged on users. The form is:

%**write lcs050**

write then accepts its input from the keyboard until **^d** is pressed; all the typing is sent to lcs050's screen. **write** is a good example of Unix's uniform way of treating devices, as it is little more than a version of **cat** that redirects to a user's terminal, which is a file in the directory **/dev**.

It is possible to stop other users interrupting you by using the **mesg** command. **mesg** without any arguments reports whether or not you will accept a message.

%**mesg n**

turns messages off.

%**mesg y**

turns them back on.

Mesg is really just a reworking of the **chmod** command. When you logon to the computer you will be allocated a line into the computer, through one of its ports. These terminal lines are files to UNIX, although files that have special pieces of software in the kernel to handle them. The terminal files are character special files in the **/dev** directory, and they are normally called tty01 to ttyn, n being the number of terminal lines your machine may have. As you you may be logged on to a different terminal line each time you login to the computer, you can use the **tty** command to find out which line you are using. The details of which particular line you are allocated will

151

depend upon the set up of your installation. **tty** responds with the path-name for your terminal file, ie:

```
%tty
/dev/tty03
```

If you look at the permissions on the file, they will be:

```
%ls -l /dev/tty03
crwx_w__w_ 1  lcs068 19, 3  Dec 23 14:08 /dev/tty03
```

The user is made owner of the file by the login process, using the **chown** and **chgrp** commands. The file has write permission for all users. Read permission is only given to the user, as other users could read what was being typed in, and this would cause many security problems.

After giving

```
%mesg n
```

we can see what has happened by looking at the file permissions again:

```
%ls -l /dev/tty03
crwx_____ 1  lcs068 19, 3  Dec 23 14:08 /dev/tty03
```

All that has happen is

```
%chmod 700 /dev/tty03
```

However the **mesg** command frees the user from having to know in advance which terminal line they are logged into. **Mesg y** does a **chmod 722** on the terminal file.

mail

UNIX has a an easy to use, intelligent mail service. The simplest thing to do is to mail another user. To mail user lcs050, type:

```
%mail lcs050
```

mail will prompt you for the mail header.

Subject:

This is used as a subject header for the message. The message is then typed in at the keyboard until **^d** is pressed, or a single line with . as its first and only character is typed. **Mail** will then prompt you:

Cc:

This means do you wish copies to be sent to other users, **Cc** means Carbon copies, if no other users are specified, then the mail is only sent to username. Here is an example mail session:

%**mail lcs050**
Subject:AWK script.88

Thanks for the AWK script, I'll try it out later today.
EOT
Cc:
%

Undelivered mail is dumped in a file called **dead.letter** in your home directory. The most common reason for mail not being delivered is that the username does not exist.

On logging in and having new mail, **mail** will prompt you with the message "You have mail". Issuing the command:

%**mail**

will give a one line header for each message you have received, giving detail of who it is from etc:

> N 1 root   tues Dec 23   14:05   "System crash"
N 2 lcs040 mon Dec 22   09:42

this is followed by a **&** prompt. If you have no messages **mail** will tell you this and quit. At the **&** prompt it is possible to:

Mail   Commands

t <message list>	type messages
n	goto and type **n**ext message
e <message list>	edit messages
f <message list>	give head lines of messages

153

d <message list>	**d**elete messages
s <message list> file	append messages to file
u <message list>	**u**ndelete messages
r <message list>	**r**eply to messages
pre <message list>	make messages go back to /usr/mail
m <user list>	**m**ail to specific users
q	**q**uit, saving unresolved messages in mbox
x	e**x**it, do not remove system mailbox
h	print out active message **h**eaders
!	shell escape
?	print this message
c [directory]	**c**hdir to directory or home if none given

A <message list> consists of integers, ranges of same, or user names separated by spaces. If omitted, Mail uses the last message typed.

A <user list> consists of user names or distribution names separated by spaces.

Distribution names are defined in .sendrc in your home directory.

The **>** points to the next message to be acted upon. The command **list** will print out a list of all available commands, but with no description of their function.

To look at a particular message the **type** command can be used. To see message number three, type:

&__type 3__

This will then type out onto the screen message number three. This could have been given as

&__t 3__

or even as

&__3__

Mail assumes that the number means that you wish to see the message.

The command

&__h__

154

will print out the headers for all the messages. If there is a large number of messages, you will only see headers for a screen full. To see the next screen, type

&z

To go back a screen, type

&z-

It is possible to step backwards and forward from the current message using + for forward and − for backward. Pressing + or − will list the next or previous message.

It is possible to view how many messages have come from a particular user. Typing

&from root

will display all the message headers from root.

If you wished to look at the first few lines of a particular message, type

&top 7

This will show the first 5 lines of message number 7, and normally includes the fields that deal with who it is from, when it was sent and its subject matter. It is possible to find out how large a message is by the size command

&size 9

will report how large message number 9 is in characters.

Ranges are specified in the form n1 − n2. To delete messages 3 through to 5, inclusive, type

&d 3 − 5

Ranges will also work for commands like **top** and **type**. Deleted mail can be recovered by using the **undelete** command. If we had mistakenly deleted message number 4 in the above command, we could recover the situation, by typing

&u 4

This will only work if we have not left the **mail** program and re-executed it since deleting the messages.

The post office is the directory **/usr/spool**. Messages are saved in files, one for each user, and the files have the same name as the user. Mail which has been read, and not deleted, is copied from the post office and appended to a file called **mbox** in the user's home directory. Deleted mail is lost once the **mail** program is exited. To stop the system from moving mail from the the system mailbox to your **mbox** file, type

&ho 6

This will hold message number 6 and leave it in the system mailbox, the command **preserve** 6 would have the same effect. Neither **hold** nor **preserve** will have any effect upon deleted messages. To stop **mail** from making any changes to the system mailbox or your mbox, type in

&ex

to exit the system.

To see what is in your **mbox** file, type

%mail -f

It is then possible to deal with the mail as one would with newly arrived mail. If you have large amounts of mail on differing subjects that you wish to keep, you can create folders to organise your mail more efficiently. Firstly create a directory to hold your folders, using the **mkdir** command, ie

%mkdir mail

Then, whilst in the mail system type

&set folder = mail

This uses the set command to inform **mail** of where your folders are to be kept. This will only work if the folder directory is in the home directory, otherwise **set folder** will have to be given as the absolute path-name of the directory. Messages can be written to folders by using the save command

&s +personal

156

This will move the current message from the **mbox** file into the folder **personal**, creating it if it does not exist, amending the message if it does. Mail can be copied across, leaving the original where it is, using the **copy** command.

&c +course

will copy the current message into the folder **course**. It is possible to view the contents of a folder by changing the current folder. To look at the folder **course**, type

&folder +course

You can then use the commands **type**, **delete** and **reply** on the folder. **Mail** can be started using a folder, ie

%mail -f personal

will run **mail** using **personal** as its start up folder. Mail can be saved from a folder into a normal file. Using

&s 3 poison .pen

will save message number 3 into the file **poison.pen**. Using the write command will do the same, except it will only save the text of the message and none of the header information that comes with mail. So to write message number 6 to the file **copy.c** type

&w 6 copy.c

Replies can be sent to message from within the mail system. **Reply** allows the user to reply to the originator, and all the recipients, of the message.

&r 4

will allow the user to reply to message number 4. **Mail** will then prompt the user in the same way as for normal mailing, except the 'To' field will be omitted. Using reply with upper case **R**, will only reply to the originator of the message, and not the recipients.

It is possible to send mail whilst within the **mail** program, using the mail command.

&m lcs040

will result in the same sequence of events as the **mail** command issued at shell level, except that control will be returned to the mail program upon termination of the message.

As is nearly always the case, the **mail** command is entered, before the message is correctly formulated, or the appropriate facts known, by the sender. Fortunately in the UNIX mail system there are a series of options still left open to the user. Following on from the above command, we could send mail to user lcs040, by typing in the following sequence:

Subject:Pascal

Dear Peter
The rates for the Pascal assignments are 25/12/86,
1/4/87.

If we realized that we had typed rates instead of dates, we could not correct the error by pressing backspace, as we had pressed return at the end of the line. It is possible to remedy this situation by using a ~ escape sequence to call up an editor. Typing

~v

on its own at the beginning of a separate line will call up the **vi** editor with the body of the message as its file. If we had typed **~e** we would have entered the **ex** editor instead. **Vi** can be used to correct the message. On exiting we will be returned to the **mail** command which will be expecting more input, or control d, to indicate end of input. If we then decided that another person should receive this message as well as lcs040, we could type

~t lcs050

As with the other ~escape commands, this must be at the beginning a line. The name lcs050 is then added to the list. The subject of the message can be changed by typing

~s MCI year II Pascal

This will change the subject header for the message from **Pascal course** to **MCI year II Pascal**. The new version of the message can be viewed by typing

~p

This would result in:

To: lcs040,lcs050
Subject: MCI year II Pascal
Dear Peter
The dates for the Pascal assignments are 25/12/87, 1/4/88.

Files can be read into the message by the **~r** command. Using

~r name.list

would result in the file name list being appended to the file, at the current line. If a copy of the file is necessary, then typing

~w Pascal.message

will write the message to the file **Pascal.message**. If we decided that we were none to sure about the date in the message, and wanted to quit mail, we would use the **cal** command to print a calendar to check the date. All of this can be done without losing the message by typing

~q

This would quit from sending mail, saving the message in the file **dead.letter**, creating a new file or overwriting the existing one. It would then be possible to check the information.

This could be done more easily within the mail system by issuing a shell escape to execute the **cal** command.

&!cal

would result in the calendar for the current year being produced on the screen. If a more complex task than a single command was required then a new interactive shell could be executed to deal with the commands. Typing

&sh

would give an interactive shell, on exiting using control d, command will be returned to the mail environment. If we then wished to return to our message, we could type:

&m
To:lcs040,lcs050
Subject:MCI year II Pascal course

We could then type

~r dead.letter

to read in the contents of the dead.letter file. The **mail** system provides a shorthand way of doing this in the command sequence

~d

this will have the same effect as the above. We could have dealt with all our problems, using **cal** etc, whilst in input mode in **mail**. The line

~!cal

would issue a shell escape to do the **cal** command. It is possible to pipe messages though a command, and replace the message with the output of the pipeline. If you wished to have the **pr** format your message then

~| pr

will use the **pr** formatter on the message, and replace the formatted version for the unformatted version. A special filter called **fmt** has been designed to format mail, to use it type

~fmt

There are a series of variables that can be changed to alter the operation of **mail**. In the above example **~v** called up the **vi** editor, however it does not have to call up **vi**. **Mail** checks the setting of the variable **VISUAL** and runs whichever editor it finds there, the default being **vi**. So if you wished **mail** to run the emacs editor instead, you would type

&set VISUAL = /usr/bin/emacs

Then when the command **~v** is entered emacs will be called up instead of **vi**. Other variables include the shell that is used in shell escapes, the variable **SHELL**, and **HOME** for an alternative home directory for the **mail** system. Rather than type these settings in anew each time **mail** is executed, it is possible to get **mail** to do them automatically for you. Commands entered into a file called **.mailrc** are automatically executed by **mail** upon execution. Here is an example **.mailrc** file:

```
%cat .mailrc
set VISUAL=/usr/bin/rand
set folder=mail
set crt=22
alias rob lcs050
alias mctutors lcs050,lcs040,lcs005
```

The third line is directing mail to pipe messages over 22 lines through **more**, so long messages will not rush by. The next two lines are setting up aliases for the mail system. These aliases are used instead of the users' names for **mail** , so from the above example, typing:

&**mail mctutors**

will be expanded by **mail** to

&**mail lcs050, lcs040, lcs005**

Other options may be set or unset in the **.mailrc** file. The lines:

unset askcc
unset ask
set toplines=12

will change one option from default and unset two other options. **Ask** and **askcc**, set up the way **mail** prompts for the subject and carbon copies (Cc). Unsetting them causes **mail** to no longer prompt for these by default. **toplines** is the number of lines displayed by the **top** command, and is 5 by default.

Many of these options can be set for all **mail** users by putting them into the file **/usr/lib/Mail.rc**. This is a system wide command file and is executed by all users using **mail**. Similarly there is a system wide aliases file. **/usr/lib/aliases** contains system wide aliases. It is updated by the **newaliases** command, which only the super-user has access to. If there are aliases that you think would be useful you should ask your system administrator to update aliases for you.

Redirection and piping can be used with the mail system.

%**mail lcs068 < message**

will mail the text in the file message to user lcs068. **Mail** will not prompt you for a subject header for the message. If you wish to give one you must use the **-s** option

%**mail -s "Social Evening" lcs068 < message**

(note the use of inverted comas for messages longer than one word).

%ls -l /bin /usr/bin /usr/ucb | grep '^-rsx' | mail root

will mail to root all the files with the 'user id bit' set in directories **/bin**, **/usr/bin** and **/usr/ucb**.

Note

The mail system discussed above is the University of California at Berkeley version, part of the Berkeley Software Distribution (**BSD**). This is located in the file **/usr/ucb/mail** and in some files in **/usr/lib**. Systems will also have the original **ATT** version of mail, which is located in **/bin/mail**. If your search path-name is altered, you may find that the ATT version **mail** becomes your default. Either change your path-name to have **/usr/ucb** before **/bin** or call the BSD mail by typing **Mail** – with an upper case M.

talk

Talk is really an interactive version of **write**. As with **write** you have to use **who** to find out if the person you wish to talk to is on the system. To talk to the user **lcc040**, type

%talk lcc040

The recipient will then receive the message:

Message from TalkDaemon@Unix
talk: connection requested by lcs068@Unix
talk: respond with: talk lcs068@Unix

on their screen. The formula **@Unix** is specifying which machine is calling, unless you intend to **talk** over the network there is no need to use this extension. In order to reply, the other user would need to type in

%talk lcs068

162

or to whichever username is calling them up. The screen will then be split into two, with a line halfway down the screen separating the two parts of the dialogue. Users just type in the text of their communication, and it is displayed on both their screen and the recipient's. The backspace and word erase keys will work as normal, and the screen can be refreshed with a control l. To end a **talk** session one or both of the users should press the interrupt key, whereupon the terminal will be reset.

Talk can be frustrated by **mesg n** being set.

msgs

Msgs is a system wide notice board. Users can send messages to the notice board, and read them. To see whether there are any messages, type

%**msgs**

This will then display headers for all the new message:

Message number 7:
From lcs068 Fri Jan 2 15:28 1987
Subject: Social evenings

Msgs will then prompt you **[ynq]**. Pressing **y** will allow you to view the message, **n** will skip to the next message, **q** will quit you out of the **msgs** system. **Msgs** will continue to prompt you with new messages until you quit or run out of message. It is possible to save messages at the prompt by typing **s**. By default it will be appended to the file **Messages** in current directory. Using the form **s filename**, will save the message in the file **filename**. The number of the message to read next is kept in a file called **.msgsrc**. In order to view messages from a particular message number, type

%**msgs 1**

This will look at all the messages on the system. Using the **-h** option allows you to see only the first part of a message.

If there are no new messages **msgs** will print

No new messages

163

Using the **-f** option can suppress this message, this is a useful option to have in your **.login** file.

To send a message to the notice board, type

%**msgs -s**

You will be prompted:

Message number 13:
From: lcs068 Mon Jan 5 10:28:01 1987
Subject: Public Domain

Entry of the message is terminated by control d. **Msgs** uses the **mail** system, and is similar to **mail** and will be easy to use for those familiar with it.

Writer's Work Bench

In this section I intend to briefly deal with the utilities that UNIX has, to help prepare and format documents.

Nroff

So far, on the section dealing with creating files, I have remained silent on how to produce high quality, formatted output. The reason for this silence is because **vi** does not offer any real formatting facilities, and is only useful for producing draft documents or program source files. In order to do any production of documents you will need the services of one of the UNIX document preparing packages. In this section I do not intend to deal with these packages in great detail. This is not to say that they are unimportant but you will probably have access to a word processing package that can meet your needs adequately. Also if you have any other books on UNIX you will probably find yourself inundated with information about UNIX text formatters.

Unlike a word processor the UNIX text formatter **nroff** is not a 'what you see is what you get' (**WYSIWYG**) package. To give an example; When you give a command to format a block of text in a word processor, you see the formatted output on the screen. With **nroff** however the formatting information is embedded into the text as a series of commands, typically beginning with a full stop '.' character. This means that you can only see what your finished text will look like when you have run it through **nroff**. The text is read and the commands are acted upon by **nroff**. Although this may sound a bit cumbersome, well actually it is, it is quite easy to produce high quality documents using **nroff**.

The **nroff** package is extremely complex and powerful. In order to give a stripped down introduction, and tell you the things you are

165

likely to need to know, I am only going to describe an **nroff** macro package. This macro package, **ms** , is a built in package of commands for indenting, justifying and generally manipulating text. Using this package will effect some non-macro **nroff** commands, however some will be useable. The **ms** commands will be signified by being in upper case, the **nroff** ones will be lower case. If you are really going to make the full use of **nroff**'s facilities then you will need to write your own macro package and get to grips with **nroff** commands.

The command to centre a line of text is:

.ce
Writer Work Bench

To underline the text simply precede it by

.ul

If you wish to underline or centre more than one line you can specify a count

.ce 4

to centre the next four lines of text. The **ms** commands **.UL** and **.CE** can be used as alternatives. If you wish to both underline and centre, then give each command on separate lines preceding the text to be formatted. It is common to want your text in paragraphs, with the text right justified. Typing

.PP

at the beginning of a paragraph will right justify your paragraphs, and begin each paragraph with a small indent. It is also common to want your paragraphs like this:

a) **To start with a non-indented character.**

b) **for each paragraph.**

To achieve this effect use:

.IP a)
text
.IP b)
text

The non-indented text can be any string of characters. It is possible to control the left margin by following the **.IP** or **.PP** by a number.

.IP a) 10

which will indent the text by ten characters. If you wish to have paragraphs without non-indented leading characters or starting indents use

.LP

The right margin can be non-justified, left ragged by using the

.NA

command Justification can be turned back on by

.AD

You may find, when processing a list or group of lines, that you don't want **nroff** to do anything to it. To stop **nroff** formatting type

.DS

Then when you have come to the end of your list, type

.DE

Nroff will start formatting again.

It is possible to control the line spacing using the **.ls** command

.ls 2

will format the text following it with double line spacing.

.ls 1

will restore single line spacing.

Blank lines or any number of blank lines can be outputted by the

.sp n

request, where **n** is the number of blank lines to be included in the output.

Page breaks can be achieved by the

.bp

command.

Documents can be given a title using the **.TL** command. Running titles can be specified as either being headers, at the top of the page, or footers, at the bottom of the page. They can also be on odd or even numbered pages. So:

.OF:Ecce Homo:Page %:Nietzsche:
.EF:Nietzsche:Page %:Ecce Homo:

is defining two footers for odd (**OF**) and even (**EF**) pages. The header and footer commands take three parameters, in the above example separated by ':' characters. In place of the ':' character, the ' can be used. These three parameters will then, respectively, be left justified, centred and right justified. The '%' symbol will be replaced in the document by the current page number. So on odd pages we would get:

Ecce Homo   **Page 3**   **Nietzsche**

and on even pages:

Nietzsche   **Page 4**   **Ecce Homo**

If the % were followed by an **i** the numeration would be Roman. Headers can be specified by using the **.OH** and **.EH** commands, with exactly the same format.

Footnotes can be included using the:

In vino veritas #
.FS #
In wine there is truth
.FE

This would then place:

 # In wine there is truth

at the bottom of the page. The # character, after the **.FS**, is optional and arbitrary. The section of text between the **FS** and **FE** can be formatted by many **nroff** and **ms** commands.

To give extra emphasis certain words or text can be printed in bold face

.B Zarathustra

To embolden the word 'Zarathustra' or:

.B
This old Saint in his forest hath not heard that God is
Dead!
.R

The text between the **.B** and **.R** is printed in bold face. To print text in *italics* use **.I**. Again **.R** will return the text to normal. These options obviously depend upon your printer being able to support such type face changes. Italics will generally come out as underlined on printers that don't support italics.

It is possible to give your document numbered headings:

.NH
The world is all that is the case.

will translate into:

1 The world is all that is the case

To have a heading without the numbers use **.SH**. **NH** can be used for more complex numbering schemes:

.NH
The world is all that is the case.
.NH 2
The world is the totality of facts, not things.
.NH 3
The world is determined by the facts, and by their
being all the facts.
.NH 3
For the totality of facts determines what is the case,
and also whatever is not the case.
....
....
.NH 2
The world divides into facts.

169

This will translate as:

1 **The world is all that is the case**
1.1 **The world is the totality of facts, not things.**
1.1.1 **The world is determined by the facts, and by their being all the facts.**
1.1.2 **For the totality of facts determines what is the case, and also whatever is not the case.**
....
....
1.2 **The world divides into facts.**

The numbers after the **.NH** tell **nroff** which level is to be incremented or started. To reset level one to one, use

.NH 0

Once you have typed some text in use **nroff** to format it:

%**nroff -ms chapter.2**

The **-ms** flag is for the particular macro package. **Nroff** will produce its output to the screen so you will have to either redirect it into a file:

%**nroff -ms tractatus >Blue book**

or pipe it to the printer:

%**nroff -ms tractatus | lpr -Pq**

Spell

UNIX also has a program that will scan a document and report upon any misspellings that it may find. This will include words it does not know, these will mainly be proper nouns.

%**spell chapter.2**

Spell will report upon the misspellings to the standard output. The default spelling is American, so it will object to labour, colour and so on. To make it check for British spellings use

%**spell -b chapter.2**

You may find it useful to ask your system administrator to add words that you use regularly to the system dictionary. This will reduce the amount of redundant output you have to pick through. The dictionary on my machine does not even know Berkeley!

look

A very useful command is **look**. This allows you to do a one off check into the spelling of a particular word, by seeing if its in the system dictionary.

%**look receive**

will report upon if it can find the word receive in the system dictionary. If it can it will report back with the word, if it can't it will remain silent. If you know the first few words, **look** will report upon the all words that have similar beginnings. To look up the word **tergiversate**, but only knowing the first few letters type

%**look tergiv**

look will report on all the word beginning with **tergiv**. The more precise the original search pattern the more it will reduce the amount of output to read.

Diction

It is possible to submit a document to the **diction** program that will check for over wordy or misused phrases. Phrases like; absolutely essential, greatly minimize, if at all possible, reason is because, will be high lighted.

Explain

If you are unsure as to whether a phrase is over wordy or not, and whether there is a shorter version **explain** can be used. **Explain** will prompt you for the phrase and report upon whether it has an alternative or not.

%explain
phrase ? absolutely essential
use essential

The output of **explain** is limited in the same way as **diction** in that it has a set of stock phrases it matches against, with a set of recommendations. Just because **explain** and **diction** do or do not like a particular phrase does not mean that its usage is or is not advisable. It does however show certain idiocies and give pointers to good usage.

Style

Finally if you feel like really submitting your outpourings to UNIX then **style** will be your final arbiter of taste. It is called:

%style chapter.4

Style will then give a readout of a vast number of statistics about your document. From various readability indexes which attempt to assess how readable a text is, based on the sizes of words correlated to the length of sentence. It will also report on the use of different parts of speech you have used, such as the number of expletives used, or how many started sentences. The output from a section of this book looked like this:

chapter.2
   readability grades:
      (Kincaid) 13.1 (auto) 14.4 (Coleman-Liau) 9.4 (Flesch)
      11.2 (53.8)
   sentence info:
      no. sent 4 no. wds 119
      av sent leng 29.8 av word leng 4.45
      no. questions 0 no. imperatives 0
      no. nonfunc wds 63 52.9%   av leng 5.78
      short sent (<25) 25% (1) long sent (>40)   0% (0)
      longest sent 37 wds at sent 3; shortest sent 21 wds at
      sent 4
   sentence types:
      simple   0% (0) complex 50% (2)
      compound 25% (1) compound-complex 25% (1)
   word usage:
      verb types as % of total verbs
      tobe 31% (5) aux 13% (2) inf 25% (4)
      passives as % of non-inf verbs   0% (0)
   types as % of total
      prep 13.4% (16) conj 3.4% (4) adv 0.8% (1)
      noun 25.2% (30) adj 17.6% (21) pron 5.9% (7)
      nominalizations 1 % (1)
   sentence beginnings:
      subject opener: noun (0) pron (0) pos (0) adj (2) art (1)
      tot 75%
      prep 25% (1) adv   0% (0)
      verb   0% (0) sub_conj   0% (0) conj   0% (0)
      expletives   0% (0)

Obviously how much sense you can make of this and how much you
want to make, will depend upon how far you are willing to pick
through your own writings. Although the indexes and statistics do not
guarantee a readable or comprehensible text, they are good at picking
out unreadable text. **Style** can best be used to keep an eye on your
literary outpouring to make sure that you are not being over
repetitive or over wordy. A worthwhile exercise would be to pass the
system documentation through these various stylistic analysis tools
and send the results to your computer supplier.

How to Compile C and Pascal Programs

You will probably find that your UNIX system comes with all manner of wonderful programming languages, from those for the practitioners of the folk arts, **fortran**, to trendy languages like **prolog**. In this section I have restricted myself to C and Pascal, as being fairly typically languages. The Pascal described is the Berkeley Pascal, which is not a particularly good implementation but it at least has the merit of being a standard version.

Compiling C programs

<u>**cc**</u> (<u>**c**</u> **c**ompiler)

UNIX has a convention that C source programs must end **.c**. If you had created a source file **trial.c**, to call the compiler type

   %**<u>cc trial.c</u>**

The compiler will then attempt to compile your program. Any error messages will be printed on the standard output (the screen). If the compilation is successful it will result in an executable file called **a.out**. This can then be run by typing

   %**<u>a.out</u>**

It is best to use the **mv** command to rename **a.out** files as they will be overwritten by ensuing successful compilations.

The diagnostic output from **cc** can be redirected into an error file

   %**<u>cc lousy.c >lousy.err</u>**

This will result in diagnostics being sent to the file **lousy.err**. An alternative to an **a.out** file for executable images can be specified with the **-o** option

  %**cc -o space space.c**

will result, on success, in the executable file **space** being created, this could be run by typing

  %**space**

If you intend use the symbolic debugger **dbx**, then a symbol table must be included in the executable image during compilation time. This can be achieved using the **-g** argument

  %**cc -g clear.c**

This will result in an **a.out** file that can be used with **dbx**.

 Other options include, **-E** which only executes the preprocessor stage of the compilation sending the source code with all its macro expansions and include files in to the screen. The **-S** option gets the compiler to produce an assembler source file. So

  %**cc -S cal.c**

will produce a file **cal.s** which will contain a source file of assembler commands. This can be quite useful if you wish to see how certain structures are implemented at lower levels in your machine's assembler. It can also be used to check how the optimalisation works, which is called with the **-O** option. This makes the compiler optimize the code generation to produce more efficient and/or compact code.

 If your source file uses any of the standard libraries then these will need to be specified on the command line. To use the standard mathematics library

  %**cc stddev.c -lm**

If you have your own libraries that you wish to include, then you must precede the **-l** argument by an **-Lpathname** argument, with the path-name of your local library.

Multiple compilations

cc can be forced to only produce object files, so that programs can be split up, compiled separately and then put together to form an executable file. If we had two modules called **mcat1.c** and **mcat2.c**, the file **mcat1.c** could be a single function that is called by **mcat2.c**. To suppress the load phase of compilation, type

%**cc -c mcat1.c**

This will produce a file **mcat1.o**. If the loading phase were not suppressed, **cc** could find errors in the code due to its relationship with **mcat2.c**. The files can be compiled and loaded together using

%**cc mcat1.o mcat2.c**

This will produce, upon success, an **a.out** file.

Make

When writing programs with multiple source and header files, it can be a big problem to know which files have been updated and which files need re-compiling. A long winded way around this is to continually recompile and relink everything. This process can be simplified by using the **make** program.

 Make is used to stress dependencies between different source and header files and to state what actions are to be done. If you had three C source files; **cal.c io.c**, **stack.c** and a header file called **cal.h**. How these are to be compiled can be specified in the make file:

    cal : cal.o io.o stack.o
       cc -o cal cal.o io.o stack.o -lm

This would be kept in a file called **makefile** or **Makefile**. This will tell **make** that the program **cal** is made of three object files **cal.o**, **io.o** and **stack.o** and that the command line to compile them should be **cc -o cal cal.o io.o stack.o -lm**. A further dependency can be introduced by:

    cal.o stack.o : cal.h

This means that both **cal.o** and **stack.o** use a file called **cal.h**. The program is called by

%**make**

This will then check to see if the file **cal** exists and whether or not any of the source or header files have been changed since the binary was produced. If they have, then the requisite modules are compiled and then relinked. So if the header file **cal.h** was changed then **make** would know enough that **cal.o** and **stack.o** need to be recompiled and then for the whole lot to be relinked.

lint

Further checking, in greater detail, can be run on C source programs using the **lint** utility. **lint** only produces diagnostic output, and does not create run time files. It will report the same syntax errors as **cc**, but **lint** will also check for portability of programs, use of system and library calls, and report on unused and uninitialised variables. To call **lint** to check the file **backward.c** type

%**lint backward.c**

Lint will produce its diagnostic output onto the screen, which can be redirected to an error file

%**lint kermit.c >kermit.err**

dbx

The Berkeley UNIX system has the **dbx** debugger which can be used to debug C programs. To call it type

%**dbx**

It will then prompt you for the executable file that it is to use, or it will use **a.out** by default. If the file has not been created by the C compiler using the **-g** option, **dbx** will warn you and cease execution. If there is a core image file, caused by the program carrying out some illegal instruction, **dbx** will attempt to read it as well. If the core file was not produced by the specified executable file, then **dbx** will ignore it.

177

Once in, **dbx** will prompt you for commands with a **(dbx)** prompt. The simplest thing to do is to list your source program

(dbx)list

The listing can be specified from a particular line, or range of lines

(dbx)list 12,24

A useful and easy thing to do is to execute the program under **dbx**'s control, which will allow you to find out which particular line it crashed out at. To execute the current program use

(dbx)run

If the program needs command line arguments, just include them on the run command line as per normal. If it requires input, then you will be prompted as under ordinary circumstances. The program will then crash, giving you a message along the lines of

(dbx)
illegal instruction in strcpy at 0x20800d8

This may then give you all the information you need to find your bug.

Further things can be done to help you debug. It is possible to set break points in the program, that is places where you wish to suspend execution and perhaps find out what has happened. To do this use the **stop at** command

(dbx)stop at 22

This will set a breakpoint at line number twenty two. The program can be run , but this time **dbx** will stop, often before the line specified, and allow you to check certain values. If you wanted to see what value a variable is set to, use the **print** command

(dbx)print pos

This will then print out the value of the variable **pos**. Structures, pointers and array variables can all be access in the same way. It is even possible to test whether or not a call to another function is successful or not. To see whether the function **strcpy** with the parameters **s1** and **s2** was successful or not type

(dbx)print strcpy(s1,s2)
strcmp returned successfully

If you wish to single step through the next few lines of code, checking values as you go, then you can use the **step**, abbreviated to **s**, command

  (dbx)s

If you wished for the program execution to continue, until the next break point, as you can have multiple breakpoints, or until termination, then use

  (dbx)cont

It is possible to get **dbx** to trace through calls to external functions, by using the **trace** command

  (dbx)trace getch

will get **dbx** to trace execution in the **getch** function.

It is possible to get **dbx** to trace variables throughout the execution of a program. Typing

  (dbx)trace i

will cause **dbx** to report on the intialisation and any changes made to the variable **i**. The changes will be reported in the form:

  (dbx)step
  after 18 : i = 3

This is not an exhaustive description of **dbx**'s facilities, to see the full list of commands type

  (dbx)help

This will give the following output:

run	**– begin execution of the program**
print <exp>	**– print the value of the expression**
where	**– print currently active procedures**
stop at <line>	**– suspend execution at the line**
stop in <proc>	**– suspend execution when <proc> is called**
cont	**– continue execution**

step	– single step one line
next	– step to next line (skip over calls)
trace <line£>	– trace execution of the line
trace <proc>	– trace calls to the procedure
trace <var>	– trace changes to the variable
trace <exp> at <line£>	– print <exp> when <line> is reached
status	– print trace/stop's in effect
delete <number>	– remove trace or stop of given number
call <proc>	– call a procedure in program
whatis <name>	– print the declaration of the name
list <line>, <line>	– list source lines
gripe	– send mail to the dbxgripe mail alias
quit	– exit dbx

Once you feel that you have run the problem to ground, then to exit **dbx** type

(dbx)quit

cb (**c** source **b**eautifier)

The **cb** program takes from standard input a C source program and produces on the standard output a correctly formatted C program.

%**cb <messy.c > wonderful.c**

will cleanup **messy.c** (read < 'as take the input from') and put the results (read > 'as put the output into') into **wonderful.c**. **Messy.c** will not be affected by this process.

180

Compiling Pascal programs

pc (**p**ascal **c**ompiler)

By convention on UNIX all Pascal source programs must end **.p**. To compile a Pascal source **first.p** type

%**pc first.p**

This will result in the diagnostic messages being sent to the standard output (the screen) and upon success an executable image file **a.out** being created. To run the **a.out** file type

%**a.out**

The diagnostic messages can be re-directed into a file using

%**pc terminal.p >terminal.err**

All diagnostics will be sent to the file **terminal.err**. Alternative object files can be specified with the **-o** argument. Thus

%**pc -o finder finder.p**

will result in the executable image file **finder** being created instead of **a.out**.

pi (**p**ascal **i**nterpreter)

UNIX also supports the University of California Berkeley (UCB) Pascal interpreter **pi**. Rather than producing an executable image, **pi** translates the source file into interpreted code to be executed by another program.

To compile a Pascal source file **new.p**, type

%**pi new.p**

If all is well, **pi** will produce a file called **obj**. This can be executed by calling the Pascal execution module

%**px**

It is advisable to use the **mv** command to rename **obj**, as it will be overwritten by later successful compilations. Typing:

> %**mv obj new**
> %**px new**

will have the same effect as **px** had above.

pix (**p**ascal **i**nterpreter and **ex**ecution module)

pix is a load and go interpreter. It will produce a temporary object file and then run it.

> %**pix new.p**

will have the same effect as:

> %**pi new.p**
> %**px**

with the only difference being **pix** will not leave an object file for later use. Both **pi** and **pix** will take a **-p** option to suppress messages. The **-l** option can be used with both to produce a listing of the file as well as the translation or execution.

All of the Pascal compilers and interpreters will do simple syntax correction. For example if a Pascal file had the line

> **for loop = 1 to 20 do**

pc, **pi** and **pix** would produce the following output:

> **8 for loop = 1 to 10 do**
> e-----------------^--- Inserted ':'**

They will then produce **a.out**, **obj** or output respectively. The correction will not be inserted into the original source program and will need to be done manually by the programmer. The number before the line is a line number, the **e** means that it is a correctable error. An **E** indicates an uncorrectable error, and **w** stands for warning.

You, History and your Environment

What happens when you login?

When a user goes through the login process, UNIX does a series of checks. Firstly it looks up your user name and checks your password in the file **/etc/passwd**. If the password field is null then the user will not be prompted for a password, and will be logged straight in. UNIX then looks in the home directory field in the file **/etc/passwd** to find out where you live, and assuming that the directory exists and you have write permission on it, it moves you there. It then starts running your shell, specified by the last field in **/etc/passwd**. If the last field is blank, then the shell **/bin/sh** is run as a default.

```
%grep "^lcs068" /etc/passwd
lcs068:&yy^~1-{Iopt:512:500:Craig Duffy:/u3/lcs/lcs068:/bin/csh
       1       2        3   4        5           6              7

The fields are:
1.  Username.
2.  Encrypted password.
3.  User id number.
4.  Group id number.
5.  General information.
6.  Home directory.
7.  Shell.
```

Figure 32. An example /etc/passwd entry

183

If you are using the **/bin/csh** shell, which you probably will be, then a file in your home directory called **.login** is executed. The **.login** file normally contains certain set up routines that you wish to have set when you login. After that a file in your home directory called **.cshrc** will be executed. This file is executed every time a new shell is spawned, whereas **.login** is executed only when a login shell is started. A login shell is only started when a shell is called through the login procedure. Running another shell can be achieved either by explicitly executing the shell, eg

    %<u>csh</u>

or

    %<u>sh</u>

It also can happen by running a shell script, or by doing a shell escape within a running program. See later on in this chapter for more details on these occurrences.

If you are using the shell **/bin/sh**, then a file in your directory called **.profile** is executed. **.profile** acts in the same way as **.cshrc**. When **csh** users logout, a file called **.logout** in the home directory is executed.

Here is an example of a **.login** file:

```
%cat .login

set history = 25
set savehist = 25
set prompt = '\!craig@`hostname` '
echo " "
/usr/games/fortune
echo " "
set ignoreeof
alias a alias
a h history
a hh "history | grep"
setenv PATH : . : /usr/ucb : /usr/bin : /bin :
stty erase ^h
mesg n
biff y
umask 077
```

History

Users of the **csh** have as part of their environment a history mechanism. This is a process whereby command lines are stored, up to a user defined limit, for re-use by the user. In order utilise this facility the user must inform the **csh** how many previous commands it is to 'remember'. This is done by setting a shell variable, called **history**, to a particular value. A common value is 25, as this means that they can all be viewed at once on a normal vdu screen. Followers of Henry "history is bunk" Ford will want **history** set to as low a value as is possible, whilst classicists and archaeologists will want substantially longer values.

After some interaction with the shell, typing the shell command **history** will list up to the last 25 commands, assuming of course that history=25.

%**history**

```
1    cat .login
2    ls -la
3    cd pascal
4    vi trial.p
5    pc trial.p -o trial.bin > trial.err
6    cat trail.err
```

The numbers on the left are the order in which the commands were typed. It is possible to recall history events from the history list. The simplest form of history recall is **!!**, this means redo the last command. Earlier events can be recalled by using the form **!number**, where number is a number from the history list; **!4** would substitute to the command **vi trial.p**. The line which sets the variable **savehist** to 25 is setting the number of command lines to be saved on logout. The command lines are saved in a file called **.savehist**, and are accessible with the **history** command when you start a new login session.

The last command can also be modified, if the line

%**cat philosophy/modern/existential/hiedegger/dasein**

was typed, with the obvious error of hiedegger instead of heidegger, then typing

^ie^ei

185

will make a correction on the previous line, and save a lot of typing. The pattern within the two **^**'s is matched in the line above, and replaced with the pattern after the second **^**. The whole line is then redone. If there had been an occurrence of **ie**, prior to the offending one, then that would have been changed in preference. So care has to be taken choosing your search/replace pattern.

Other incantations of **!** can be used. **!$** means the last word from the above line. thus with:

%**vi terminal1.c**
%**cc terminal2.o !$**

the **!$** on the second line would be replaced with the name **terminal1.c**, and would execute

%**cc terminal2.o terminal1.c**

The form **!^** picks the first argument, so

%**mv !^ terms.o**

would result in the line

%**mv terminal2.o terms.o**

being executed. The form **!*** picks out all the arguments from **!^** to **!$**. Typing

%**diff letter.1 letter.2**

followed by

%**spell !***

would result in the line

%**spell letter.1 letter.2**

being executed.

The form **!character(s)**, can be used to pick the most recent occurrence of the command line starting with character(s). In the above example if **!v** were used the command line **vi terminal.c** would be executed. Care has to be taken, as the shell will pick the first match, and you may need to use more characters to differentiate between different commands.

Commands can be picked from selected lines using **!number : nfrom-nto**. The arguments of a command line start at 0. So with the commands:

%<u>cat /etc/passwd</u>
%<u>who | grep '^cs' | wc -l</u>
%<u>history</u>
     8 cat /etc/passwd
     9 who | grep '^cs' | wc -l
     10 history
%<u>!8 !9:1-6</u>

the command line **!8 !9:1-6** recalls all of event 8 , and **!9:1-6** recalls commands 1 to 6 from event 9. This would result in

cat /etc/passwd | grep '^cs' | wc -l

Note that the pipe character, and the redirection characters, **>**, **>>** and **<**, all count as one command.

Events can be selected and edited using history substitutions, for example:

%<u>history</u>
     1 grep '^mc' /etc/passwd | awk -F: '{ print $1 }'
     2 cat my.message
     ....
     12 history
%<u>!1:s/mc/lc/</u>

the last line will recall event number 1, **!1**, and will do a substitution on the first occurrence of **mc** it meets, changing it to **lc**. So the line

grep '^lc' /etc/passwd | awk -F: '{ print $1 }'

would be executed. The pattern **/mc/lc/** can be followed by **g** to make the change globally throughout the whole line.

In the example of a **.login** file, the second line has

set prompt = '\!craig @`hostname` '

187

This changes the system prompt from % to **craig @ machine** (the **\!** translates into 'replace with the current history event number'), where machine is the name of the machine returned by the **hostname** command. The format

    `` `hostname` ``

is quite interesting. The command **hostname** simply returns the network name of the machine that the command is executed on. So if we typed

    %<u>hostname</u>

on the machine **sol** it would return the name **sol**. The grave `` characters are special shell characters. They tell the shell to do the command and then replace in the input line the command's output. So typing

    %<u>echo The date is `` `date` `` on `` `hostname` ``</u>

would return

    The date is Tues Jun 5 12:03:43 GMT 1991 on sol

So the command **echo** received the output from the **date** and **hostname** commands on its command line. This means that using the format **'\!craig@`hostname`** ', on logging in the user will have this prompt

    1craig@sol

indicating that the history is at 1. After the tenth command the prompt will be

    11craig@sol

If we **rlogin** to another machine, **zugzwang** for example then the prompt would become

    1craig@zugzwang

The lines three, four and five of the **.login** file:

```
echo " "
/usr/games/fortune
echo " "
```

use the **echo** command to echo a blank line, followed by the **fortune** command (which results in a random adage being printed on the screen), followed by another blank line. It is possible to include most UNIX commands and pipe lines in **.login**, such as **date**, **who** etc. However some people find that watching this verbiage go by for 1/2 an hour a trifle pointless.

Shell variables

When you login, a command line interpreter, the shell, starts running to deal with your commands. The two most common are the **csh** and **sh** shells. The **sh**, also known as the Bourne shell after Steve Bourne who wrote it, is the original shell from UNIX Edition 7. The **csh**, which was written by Bill Joy at the University of California at Berkeley, is called the C-shell as it attempts, wherever possible, to use the same command syntax as the C programming language. The relative merits of the two shells is a subject that brings out the theological in many UNIX users, and consequently an arcane controversy has revolved around this subject.

The major difference apart from the differing command syntax and the odd command, is that the **csh** loads a hashed table of commands from the search path upon execution and the **sh** does not. This means that the **csh** is slower at start up time, with the overhead of hashing and loading up such a table. The **sh** has no such problems, but it is slower at command execution as it has to search the path each time for commands. Being the original shell, **sh** has been used much longer and it is the favoured language for writing shell scripts, programs written in the shell language. The **csh** is the most popular, being very strong on useful interactive features, such as **history**, and is easy to use. There is even a command, called **chsh**, on many systems which allows users, of catholic tastes, to switch from the Bourne to the C-shell and vice versa. This section will mainly be of relevance to **csh** users, which will probably be most users.

Each shell has a set of variables initialised when it is started, these are useful things it needs to know, for example; the name of the user, the home directory of the user. Most of these variables are accessible to the user, and can be set to alter the user's environment. Much of the burden of **.login**, .cshrc and **.profile** is the setting up of these shell variables.

Csh variables are of two kinds local and global, as will be explained later on. The line, from **.login**

> **set ignoreeof**

is setting up a local environment variable. This particular one stops **^d** from logging the user off the system. Some of the environment variables are toggled, such as

> %<u>**set verbose**</u>

which sets the **csh** to verbose mode, meaning that the shell will echo all of it arguments, plus all substitutions, before executing the command. Other variables are set to a particular value, eg. **history=25**. The variable **biff** which is set to **y**, which means on or yes, controls whether the **mail** program can interrupt and warn of mail messages that have arrived.

The line

> **umask 077**

is setting up a file creation mask. When files are created they must have default read, write and execute permissions set. The **umask** variable changes that setting. The value **umask** is set to does a logical not on the permission bits – so 077 would always create files with

> **rwx_____**

permissions. Seven blanks out all of the permissions. So **umask** 666 (the mask of the beast?) would create

> **rw_rw_rw_**

permissions on file creation.

To find out what variables you have set type

> %<u>**set**</u>

This reports on all your variables and their settings.

To look at particular variable settings the **echo** command can be used. **Echo** normally just echoes its arguments onto the terminal screen. The line

> **%echo "hi there"**

will result in the words "hi there" being echoed on the screen, the quotes are optional. If words are prefixed by a **$** then the shell will substitute any variable settings they may have, and **echo** will print them out on the screen. To find out the setting of your path variable, type

> **%echo $path**

To access unknown variables is an error in the **csh**, and although nothing is echoed with the **sh**, it is not an error.

The sequence:

> **%set ascii="""cat /usr/pub/ascii"**
> **%echo $ascii**

will result in the command line **cat /usr/pub/ascii** being echoed on the screen. The variables can be used as shorthand command names. So by typing

> **%$ascii**

will cause the command line **cat /usr/pub/ascii** to be executed – this will give you a map of the ascii character set.

The command **unset** removes the association of a variable name and value.

So

> **%unset verbose**
> **%unset ascii**

will turn off verbose mode, and stops **$ascii** being associated with the command line **cat /usr/pub/ascii**.

All variables that are set up using the form **set var** or **set var=value** are only local to your shell; if you change your shell, these values are lost.

Global variables are generally in upper case, and are set up using the **setenv** (**set env**ironment) command. These take the form **setenv variable_name value**. To see what global variables have been set type

%printenv

this will show all current variable settings. To change the setting of the TERM variable to d0 (DEC VT100) type

%setenv TERM d0

The global variables can also be accessed by using the **$variable_name** format. Global variables can be removed by using the form **unsetenv variable_name**. To unset the variable TERM type

%unsetenv TERM

You can see the difference between local and global variables by trying this example.

Set up a local variable, by typing in the line

%set local="my shell"

Then set up a global variable, ie type in the line

%setenv GLOBAL "any shell "

Enter **vi** and then issue a shell escape. This forces **vi** to execute a new shell to deal with the command line. The new shell will initialise its own variables. If you then issue commands to look at these variables:

:!set

and:

:!printenv

you will see that your local (lower case) variable is no longer known to the new shell, whereas your global (upper case) variable is known. The global variable has, in UNIX terminology, been exported to the new shell.

Some variables, both local and global, such as path, home, prompt, shell, etc are initialised on entry into each shell.

If you use the Berkeley ARPA **rsh** command you should put this line right at the beginning

> **if !($?prompt) then**
> **exit**
> **endif**

into your **.cshrc** file. This tests to see whether an interactive shell is being executed, if it is not then the **.cshrc** is aborted. This means that when running a command line like

> %rsh <u>vega df</u>

the **.cshrc** file will not go through a whole series of initialisation routines. The command is using the **csh**'s built-in **if** statement which is testing for the non-existance, !, of the variable **prompt**, **$?prompt**. If **prompt** does not exist the **then** statement is executed, **exit**, otherwise the rest of the **.cshrc** file is executed.

Alias Thompson and Ritchie

The line, in **.login**

> **alias a alias**

is using the **csh alias** system. It is invoked by using the form:

> **alias alias_name   command name**

Making **alias** the first alias is a common way of avoiding a large amount of typing. If the command **alias** is typed in on its own – or the aliased **a** in this case – then all the current aliases will be listed. Notice that command pipe lines can be used. **alias hh "history | grep"** will allow the history list to be passed through grep to search for certain occurrences.

> %<u>hh vi</u>

will search the history list for all uses of the command **vi**. This would result in

> **history | grep vi**

being executed.

Primos fans can replicate their Primos environment with such aliases as:

> %**alias pop cd ..**
> %**alias ld ls -a**

Or MS-DOS could be duplicated with:

> %**alias type cat**
> %**alias dir ls**
> %**alias copy cp**

and so on. History substitutions can be used in aliases:

> **alias cd 'set prev=$cwd;chdir \!*'**
> **alias ret 'set ret=$prev;set prev=$cwd;cd $ret;unset**
> **prev;pwd'**

These two aliases are quite complex and need some explaining. **Cd** is changing the **cd** command so that it keeps, in the variable **$prev**, a record of the last directory. The variable **$cwd** keeps the path-name of the current working directory. The **Chdir** command is used, in preference to the **cd** command, as it is illegal to use the aliased name in the actual definition of the alias.

The command **ret** returns the user back to the previous directory. It uses a temporary variable **ret** to store the previous directory name. It then records the current working directory, as this will be the previous directory after the **cd**. It then changes directory, removes the temporary variable and prints out the working directory, **pwd**.

Aliases can be switched off by using the **unalias** command. So

> %**unalias a**

would remove **a** from the alias list.

Command paths

In the example **.login** file the command line

> **setenv PATH : . : /usr/ucb : /usr/bin : /bin:**

is included. This sets up a global path variable. The **path** and **PATH** variables are set up by default by the shell, but can be tailor made for particular users. The **PATH/path** variables map out the search path for the shell when executing commands. The '.' entry in the path refers to the current directory. This means that it is possible to create executable commands in the current directory. The accessibility of the path variables allows users to write their own front ends for UNIX, filtering or replacing system commands through their own commands. If you found the **clear** command (clear the screen) too slow, the you can write your own version of it. Typing

>   **echo "esc : "**

into a file called **clear** and changing the mode of the file to 755, to make it executable . <u>**Note:** **this will only work on some terminals.**</u>
It is common for users to include the line

>   **$HOME/bin**

in their search path, and to put all of their own binaries in their own **bin** directory. Then when you enter the command **clear**, your version will be executed in preference to the system version. For users of the **csh** it will be necessary to enter the command

>   **%<u>rehash</u>**

as the **csh**'s hashed list of commands will need updating in order to tell the **csh** about this new command. This is only necessary when you wish to execute a command from your search path, so if you executed it directly by typing out the full path-name of the command, rehashing would not be necessary. It is not necessary to issue rehash every time you wish to use the command as the **csh** will get the updated version on next login.

Setting up your terminal

You may find that when working with your terminal it does not always respond as it should. Sometimes this will be due to hardware faults or transmission errors. However, many times it will be due to the software settings that UNIX has for your terminal. These settings can be changed using the **stty** (<u>s</u>et <u>tty</u>)command. **Stty** is a UNIX utility not a shell built in and is used to set and reset the characteristics of tty lines. The line in the **.login** file

>**stty erase erase ^h**

sets the shell to accept **^h** (control h) as the erase character. To find out all the current settings type

>%<u>stty all</u>

This will result in something like this:

new tty, speed 9600 baud; -tabs

erase	kill	werase	rprint	flush	lnext	susp
^h	^?	^w	^r	^o	^v	^z/^y

intr	quit	stop	eof
^c	^\	^s/^q	^d

Some of the setting are toggled

>%<u>stty -echo</u>

will turn off character echoing, and everything that is typed on the screen will no longer be echoed. This option is used by the **passwd** program to stop the user's password being echoed on the terminal screen.

If you log in on a terminal that has shift/alpha lock depressed, then UNIX will assume that your terminal can only accept upper case characters. This effectively executes the command

>**stty lcase**

which means 'map all lower case characters on to upper case ones'. To reset this, so as to accept lower case characters, type

>%<u>stty -lcase</u>

Some other **stty** settings are to do with which characters you wish to have special meaning to UNIX. If you wished to stop **^z** being associated with suspending jobs, the line

>%<u>stty susp ^u</u>

would make **^u** the suspend control character. **^y** is the delayed suspend character and is changed with the command line **stty dsusp**.

UNIX utilities, such as **vi** and **more**, need to known certain information about the user's terminal, such as how many columns and lines it has, what is underline mode and so on. These utilities find out about these things from a file called **/etc/termcap**. **/etc/termcap** is a data base of terminal entries and it hopefully contains information about all the terminals that UNIX may meet. The entries are of the format:

d0 | vt100 | vt100-am | dec vt100:
:cr=^M:do=^J:nl=^J:bl=^G:co#80:li#24:kb=^h:

The first character string, **d0**, is used to reference the differing entries. It is followed by the name and make and model of the terminal, plus any other useful information, such as other look alikes, near misses and so on.

The rest of **termcap** explains, in one long string, differing aspects of the terminals behaviour. Each entry is separated by colons :, and is normally of the form **XX=YY**. For example it describes the key stroke required to do cursor movements; **cr**, carriage return is control m; **do**, control J is cursor down and new line (nl); **bl**, control G, rings the bell on the terminal; **li**, the number of lines is 24; **co**, the number of columns is 80; and so on.

Utilities find out about which terminal is being used through the variables **TERM** and **term**. This is set to a character string that references with a terminal description in **/etc/termcap**. The system administrator will take an educated guess as to what terminal the users will meet and put them in a file called **/etc/ttytype** . This gives the shell its default setting.

Users can access the **TERM** and **term** variables in the standard ways. If you know that you are always going to use a particular terminal and it is not the default setting, then you can put your favoured setting in your **.login** file.

It is possible to see what your termcap settings are by using the **tset** command. The line

%<u>tset</u>

will report, with a termcap styled report, on your terminal's particular settings.

Due to the multiplicity of different terminals and different versions of particular terminals, **/etc/termcap** can be wrong. It is possible to

197

use your own local version of termcap to test out different terminal settings. This is achieved by using the global variable **TERMCAP**, either set to the path-name of your own termcap file, or set to a string that is a termcap styled entry.

Running jobs in the background

Some jobs may take a long time to run and hold up the terminal while you sit there doing nothing. These jobs can be run in the background forcing a new shell to do the work and liberating your login shell for interactive work. For example, if you wished to use the **find** command to search the system for core dump files and put their location into a file, use

%find / -name core -print >>core.report

The slash (/) tells **find** to search from root – ie look everywhere; -**name** specifies the file **core** to be searched for; -**print** specifies for **find** to report the path-names of core files found, and the output redirects into a file called **core.report**. (For more information on **find** consult the manuals – **man find**).

This search could take some time. If you typed

%find / -name core -print >>core.report &
12867

the trailing **&** sign tells UNIX that the job is to be run in the background. The shell supplies us with a process number – the number **12867** in this case. This can be used if we wish to stop the job using the kill command. To stop it type the line

%kill 12867

otherwise the shell will report upon the job, either when it has finished or run into an error and had to stop.

Jobs that are in the foreground can also be suspended by pressing **^z** or **^y**. When one of these has been pressed the shell will report

stopped

and the job will be entered onto a list of background and stopped jobs. To examine this list type

%**jobs**

Some of the jobs will be suspended, others running in the background. Each job has a number in front of it, which can be used with the **kill** % command. If **jobs** produced the list:

[1] **stopped**   **man man**
[2] **running**   **find / -name core -print >>corefile**
[3] **stopped**   **lint kermit.c >kermit.err**

then:

%**kill %3**

would kill the command line **lint** etc...

The job at the top of the list can be killed off with the form

%**kill %%**

Alternatively these jobs can be killed by finding their process numbers, using **ps -l**, and **kill process_no.** Typing

%**ps -l**

will call **ps**, the process status command, with the **-l** option which forces it to give a long listing. The output from the above will be:

F	UID	PID	PPID	CP	PRI	NI	ADDR	SZ	RSS
4092	12	987	876	0	15	0	4f	56	44

WCHAN	STAT	TT	TIME	COMMAND
6543	S	09	0:32	find / ...

Much of the information given is details of what the process is doing, where it is doing it and so. The column **UID** gives the user id of the user running the process, **PID** gives the process number of the process, **PPID** is identification number of the parent of the process, ie the process that started it running. To kill off a job simply find its process id. So to kill off the job **find......**, type in

%**kill 987**

199

Care should be taken not to kill off the process **csh**, or the **PPID**, parent process id, as these could result in you being logged off the system.

If a job refuses to be killed, use the -9 option, ie

%<u>**kill -9 19888**</u>

This means that the process cannot ignore the signal and will have to die. It is not possible to kill off other users' processes, unless you are super user.

It is possible to make jobs difficult to kill by running them with the **nohup**, no hang up, option. Typing

%<u>**nohup find / -name core -print >>core.report &**</u>
1274

will mean that job number 1274 can only be killed with the -9 option, and will not die on termination of its parent process, namely the process which started it, the shell. This means that this job will keep going after the user has logged out.

Jobs in the background and on the suspended job list can be brought back to life or into the foreground using the **fg** (**fore**ground) command. Thus

%<u>**fg %3**</u>

would bring job number 3 back to life again, and stop the shell from accepting interactive input. The top job on the list can be brought into the foreground by typing

%<u>**fg**</u>

Jobs can be restarted without the **fg** command. In fact just naming a job by typing

%<u>**%2**</u>

will bring it into the foreground, ie bringing job number 2 into the foreground.

Jobs that have been suspended can be restarted in background mode by the **bg** (**b**ackground) command. **bg** with no arguments restarts the job at the top of the list, or jobs can be specified as in

    %bg %4

which will startup job number 4.

Changing .login, .cshrc and .profile

You might be slightly surprised to notice that the **.login**, **.cshrc**, **.logout** and **.profile** files do not usually have execute permission set, nor need it set for them to work. You may also be frustrated in your efforts to make amendments to these files, and then executing them to see if your changes have worked. Even changing the permissions to include execute does no good, as they can be executed but the changes will not register in the current environment.

What is needed, in the case of the **csh**, is to type

    %source .login

or **.cshrc**, for whichever file. If you use the **-h** option it will save all of the command lines executed in your history list as if you had typed them in at the shell prompt. For the **sh**, type

    %. .profile

This will mean that the changes you have made will be reflected in your current environment. It is interesting to see why simply executing the files has no effect.

When the shell is called to execute different files, it takes certain actions. After finding out whether or not the command exists and whether or not your permissions are okay, the shell then tries to figure out what kind of file it is. If it is an executable binary file, that has been produced by a compiler, the shell executes it directly. Unless told otherwise by the **&** operator, the shell will wait until the program has finished executing, and then return with the prompt and perhaps a message about the status of the program's execution.

If the file is an ascii text file, then it is assumed to be a shell script. If the shell being used is the **csh** it will check the first character in the file to see if it is a **£**. If it is, then it is taken to be a **csh** script, otherwise it is assumed to be a **sh** script. Whichever type it is, the shell will then call the appropriate shell with the file as its command input. This means that the shell runs a new version of the shell, and therefore any change made by that command input will be local, unless any global settings are made, to the new shell. When execution has concluded, control is then returned to the calling shell, and the new settings are forgotten. The **source** command in the **csh** and doing . in the **sh** causes the current shell to take the command file as it own input, and therefore for any changes to take effect on the login shell.

The tenex style shell

On many UNIX systems there is a new version of the **csh** available. It is known as the tenex style shell. It can either be invoked by setting an option within the **csh** or by calling a new command line interpreter.

In the former case, typing

> %**set tenex**

will set up the tenex option. In the latter case it is necessary to execute the new shell by

> %**tcsh**

If you wish to set up your own environment you will need to create a file, in your home directory, called **.tcsh**. You will also need to contact your system administrators as they will have to alter your shell entry in the file **/etc/passwd**.

The tenex shell is compatible with the **csh** but it also contains some new features for file, history, user and command substitution, as well as advanced command line editing. The line editing makes it closer to **VAX VMS** command line editing on a VT100+ terminal.

It is easier to step through history lists. **^p (previous-command)** re-invokes onto the current line the previous history event(s). **^n (next-command)** step forward through the history list. It is necessary to have stepped backward through the history list before one can step forward through it, for obvious reasons. Also it is necessary to have set **history** to a value on login.

The command lines can be manipulated with certain control key strokes. **^f (forward-character)** and **^b (backward-character)** move forward and backward, respectively, one character at a time, through the command line. **^g (forward-word)** and **^h (backward-word)** moving forward and backward one word at a time. **^a (start-of-line)** and **^e (end-of-line)** will move the cursor to the beginning and end of the command line. So with a history list like this:

%<u>history</u>
1 cat .tcsh
2 vi .tcsh
3 mail root
4 history

pressing **^p** 3 times, followed by **^h**, **^b**, would leave the cursor on the **v** of **vi**.

The command lines can be edited using key strokes. **^? (delete-char-backward)** or **DEL** will backspace and delete one character at a time. **^d (logout-or-delete-char-forward)** will delete one character forward, or if the line is empty give the **EOF** signal. **^o (delete-word-forward)** and **^w (delete-word-backward)** will delete one word forward or backward. **^k (kill-to-end-of-line)** will delete from the current cursor position to the end of line, whilst **^u (kill-to-start-of-line)** will delete to the beginning of line. The entire line can be deleted by typing **^x (kill-line)**. **^r (retype-line)** retypes the command line. After a command line has been edited, or re-invoked, it can be submitted to the shell for execution by carriage return.

It is possible to get the shell to give you a list of alternatives for command names. Pressing **^l (list-candidate)** on an unfinished command line will give you the alternative endings the shell can find for the line. For example

%<u>lo</u>

with **^l** pressed at the end of it would give

lock login logout look

If either the partial command line is unambiguous or the user types the next letter(s) to make it unambiguous, the **tcsh** can complete the line. Pressing escape or **^[(expand)** will cause the command line to be completed. If

%<u>loo</u>

was typed, followed by escape, the **tcsh** would complete the line, giving you **look**. If the **tcsh** cannot find a match or the match is ambiguous, it will beep at you.

Typing a space followed by **^l** will list all the commands on the system.

Similar expansions can be used for files and users. Typing

%<u>ls ~en</u>

followed by **^l** will result in all the users' names beginning **en** being listed. Again unambiguous users' names can be completed by escape. Typing

%<u>~</u>

followed by **^l** will report on all the users on the system. File names can be expanded in a similar way.

It is possible to reassign commands to different key strokes by using the **bind** command. Typing

%<u>**bind forward-character ^c**</u>

will make the forward character key strokes **^c**. The rather verbose names in the brackets I have give after each command key are to be used in the **bind** statement. The full list of command names is under the manual entry for **tcsh**. To stop the **tcsh** from interpreting the key strokes, you can type **^v (literal-next)**, this forces it to take the next character literally and not act upon it. These setting can be removed by binding the character to **undefined**, ie

%<u>**bind ^c undefined**</u>

The binds can be reset to their default settings by typing **bind default**.

The EMACS Editor

On many systems you may have a choice of editors. This choice, like many others in the UNIX arena, is a mine-field of conflicting pressure groups. Two of the most vociferous are the **VLF** (**vi** liberation front) and the **HJFE** (holy jihad for **emacs**). Just by putting **emacs** into bold type has probably already caused a fatawa to be placed on my life. Such are the perils of programming. These problems aside, the **emacs** editor, developed by Richard Stallman at Massachusetts Institute of Technology has been ported to a wide variety of machines, from mainframes to micros. It is available as Public Domain software and there is an all-singing all-dancing version freely available from Richard Stallman's Free Software Foundation. The later version is called **GNU emacs**, with GNU standing for **G**nu is **N**ot **U**nix (work it out for yourselves!). If you can persuade your system manager/administrator to put it on your system you won't regret it!

In this section I intend to give a brief introduction to the workings of microemacs. This is a widely available stripped down version of **emacs** which is, generally, compatible with other emacses. The editor is called up by the command name

    %<u>emacs</u>

or to create a new file or open an existing one

    %<u>emacs swann</u>

This will result in the display given below. The screen is broken into different regions: the main text entry/display part, called a window; a status bar, below the window, for information display; and at the bottom of the screen a one line mini-buffer for entering commands. The status bar will normally display information about the name of the current file being displayed, andwhether or not the current data buffer has been changed and not saved to disc. You may notice that on some of the emacs examples given later in this chapter that there is

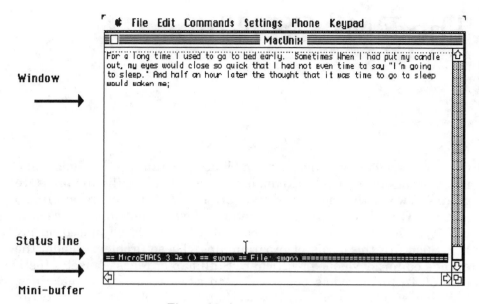

Window

Status line

Mini-buffer

Figure 33. An emacs screen

an asterisk * on the bottom left hand side of the status bar, this indicates that the text has been changed. The status bar will also display information about any special mode that is currently being used; for example if the data being edited were a C program that edit session would operate in C-mode.

Simple commands – essential emacs

The simplest things that any editor provides are the keystrokes which allow you to reposition the cursor at points in the text. To move up and down one line of text at a time use **^n** and **^p** respectively. Single character movement is achieved with **^f** and **^b** for, you guessed it, character forward and character back; using **esc b** (escape) and **esc f** will move backward and forward one word. Scrolling up and down the screen is done with **^v** and **esc v**. Moving to the top and bottom of complete files is done via the **esc <** and **esc >** commands.

Unlike **vi**, **emacs** is always in data entry mode, and all commands are either preceded by pressing the escape key or by pressing the key

206

at the same time as the control key. There are two types of command within **emacs**: bound commands and mini-buffer commands. Bound commands are commands that have been bound to particular key strokes; eg **^L** for refresh screen, or **^a** and **^e** for goto start or end of line respectively. Mini-buffer commands are entered by calling up the mini-buffer prompt by the command **esc x** this results in a **:** prompt in the minibuffer. The command name can then be typed into the mini-buffer: these can either be the names of commands that are already bound or the names of unbound commands. If we wished to use the **goto-line** command, which is unbound on my system I would have to type in **esc x goto-line**

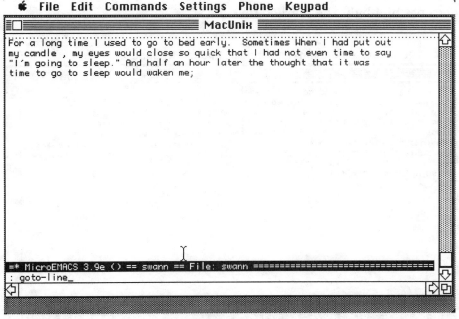

Figure 34

If the command requires any parameters, for example which line to goto, then they will be prompted for in the mini-buffer. Later on in this chapter we shall see how commands can be bound or rebound to keys on start-up or during an edit session.

207

Characters can be deleted by using a variety of keystrokes, the simplest is to use the backspace key. Using **^d** will delete the character the cursor is on, whilst **esc d** will delete the current word. Whole lines can be deleted, from the current point to the end of line using **^k**. However it is often the case that you wish to delete, copy or move larger units of text. In order to do this it is necessary to place a mark within the text. This is achieved by using either **esc space** or **^@**. This will result in the message 'mark set' in the mini-buffer. Then the cursor must be moved to the end of the piece of text to be moved or copied.

In the piece of text displayed below if the mark is set on the start of the final sentence '*I would ..*' and the cursor placed at the end of that sentence. This section of text is now marked – unfortunately **emacs** does not highlight the marked text.

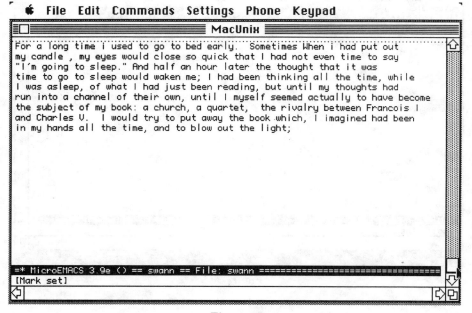

Figure 35

If you ever get confused as to where your mark is it is possible to use the **^x^x** command which exchanges the current point for the mark. Once you have the pointer and mark set around the required text the command **^w** will move it into the yank buffer or **esc w** will make a copy of it into the yank buffer. The yank buffer is a hidden buffer where text that is yanked (cut) or copied is placed. Using **^w** on the above text would have given us

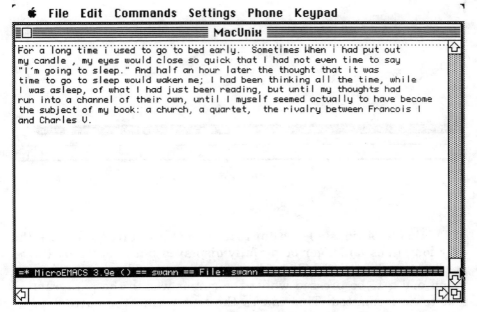

Figure 36

The cursor can then be moved to the correct place in the text for the yanked text to be moved/copied to. Then **^y** can be pressed to yank the text back out into the new position. In the displayed example, if the cursor is placed just after the words *'waken me'* , it would give the result shown below. It is possible to re-yank the text out of the paste buffer, and it can be yanked out as many times as desired. If some new text is cut into the paste buffer, then that text will become the text that is yanked out on using **^y**. The previously yanked text will be lost.

209

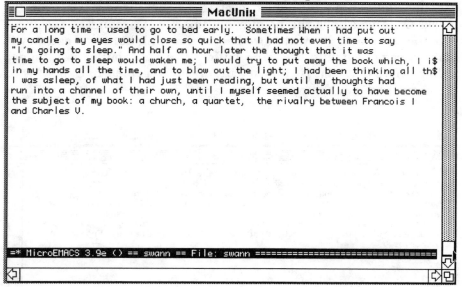

```
MacUnix
For a long time i used to go to bed early.  Sometimes When i had put out    ⇧
my candle , my eyes would close so quick that I had not even time to say
"I'm going to sleep." And half an hour later the thought that it was
time to go to sleep would waken me; I would try to put away the book which, I i$
in my hands all the time, and to blow out the light; I had been thinking all th$
I was asleep, of what I had just been reading, but until my thoughts had
run into a channel of their own, until I myself seemed actually to have become
the subject of my book: a church, a quartet,   the rivalry between Francois I
and Charles V.




=* MicroEMACS 3.9e () == swann == File: swann =============================
```

Figure 37

This could obviously leave our text in quite a scruffy state, with the over long lines no longer being fully displayed but denoted by the $s at the end of the lines. To reformat the text would require the command **esc q** to be pressed whilst the cursor was in the paragraph of text to be formatted. This causes the text within the current paragraph to be reformatted. The number of columns, ie the number of characters displayed per line, can be reset by using **^xf**, the fill-column command. This will either take a numeric argument, by preceding it with **esc 80**, or whatever the number of columns you want, or by placing the cursor in the actual column you want to justify to and then typing **^xf**. The normal default size for fill-column is 79. The result of doing a **esc q** on our example text would be:

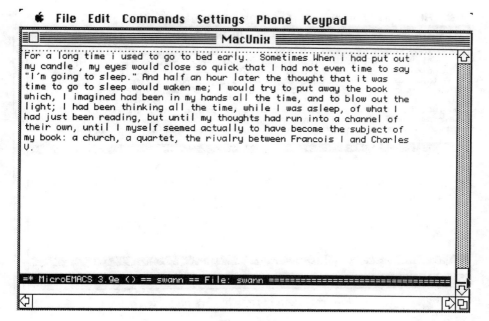

For a long time i used to go to bed early. Sometimes When i had put out
my candle , my eyes would close so quick that I had not even time to say
"I'm going to sleep." And half an hour later the thought that it was
time to go to sleep would waken me; I would try to put away the book
which, I imagined had been in my hands all the time, and to blow out the
light; I had been thinking all the time, while I was asleep, of what I
had just been reading, but until my thoughts had run into a channel of
their own, until I myself seemed actually to have become the subject of
my book: a church, a quartet, the rivalry between Francois I and Charles
V.

=* MicroEMACS 3.9e () == swann == File: swann ===============================

Figure 38

Buffers, files and windows

In **emacs** it is possible to be working on more than one file at once.
Each file that is being worked on has a buffer associated with it. The
buffer normally has the same name as the file being worked upon.
Sometimes, when working on files from different parts of the directory structure with the same name, it is necessary to give the buffer a
distinct name – but don't worry about this as **emacs** will prompt you
under these circumstances. It is possible to view a list of all the buffers in use by **^x^b** this opens another window with a listing of information about buffers.

211

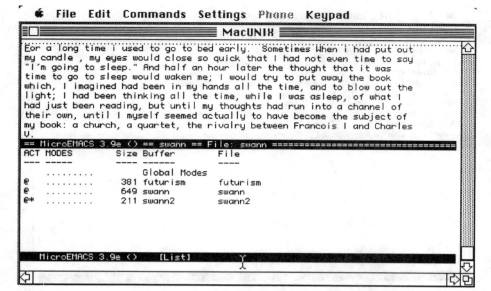

*Figure 39. An **emacs** buffers menu list*

This also shows another **emacs** feature, the ability to display more than one window at once. Running the display-buffers command splits the screen and displays the buffer listing. If the buffer listing is longer than the window size, it is possible to scroll the other window without leaving the current one using **esc ^v**. It is possible to remove that window by using the **^x1** command. This command makes the current window the only window. The command **^x2**, splits the screen and creates another window onto the current buffer. It is possible to then use the **^xo** command to change to the other window (**^xp** changes back to the previous window) and then issue a **^x^f** command to read a new file into that buffer.

Emacs can display more than two windows, and it is possible to continually spilt the windows until there are a series of one character high windows! It is possible to resize the windows by using the **^x^** window grow command or **^x^z** window shrink command.

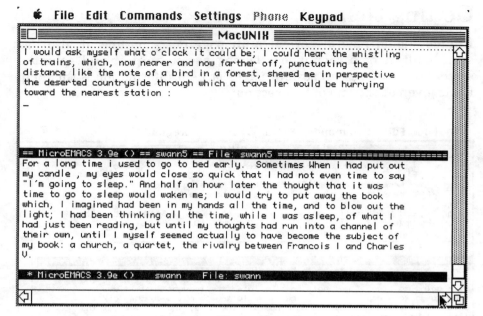

Figure 40

Moving from one buffer to another can be achieved using the **^xb** command, this prompts in the minibuffer for a buffer name, and it will either change to that buffer or create it. If you do create a new buffer and type data into it, it is worth remembering that it is only a buffer and not a file. If you quit out of **emacs** it will not warn you that you have not saved the data to a file as it is not a buffer associated with a file. To associate a buffer with a file you can either read the file into the buffer – **^x^r** , or write the buffer to a file – **^x^w**. The filenames will be prompted for in either case, using **^x^r** will overwrite the buffer with the named file.

Buffers can be deleted when no longer used by the **^xk** command, this will prompt for the name of the buffer to be deleted.

It is possible to insert files without overwriting the current contents using **^x^i** this will then prompt for a file name, the contents of which will be inserted starting from the current cursor position.

Getting Help

Emacs should have a normal **man** page entry on-line, it also has some built-in help commands. Typing **esc x help** should split the screen and through up several pages of help information – this help file is given at the end of this section.

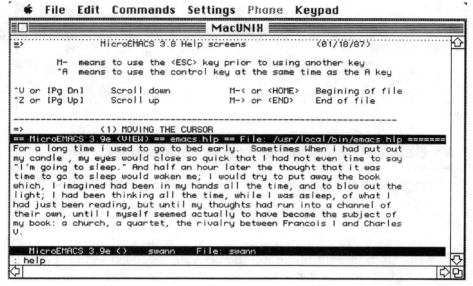

Figure 41

If you wish to find out the key binding or name of a command you can use the apropos command, **esc a**. This will prompt for a command name or part of a command name and it will then list all of the commands with that name and their known key bindings. So if we wanted to find out what the command to delete a buffer was, all we would need to type was **esc a delete Emacs** would respond with the split screen shown below. The names given along with the key bindings can be used in the minibuffer – so to delete a buffer you could either press **^xk** or **esc x delete-buffer**. It is possible to find out what command is bound to a key sequence by using **^x?** this will prompt for a key sequence and will report back what command is bound to that sequence; so typing **^x?esc z** would report back quick-exit. This later command writes the buffer(s) to file and exits without prompting.

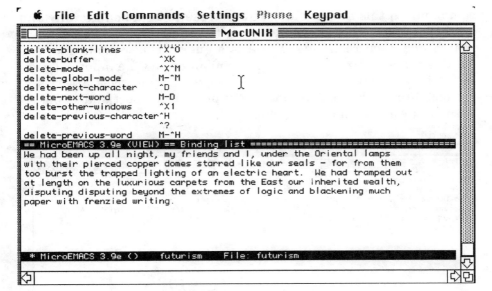

MacUNIX

```
delete-blank-lines          ^X^O
delete-buffer               ^XK
delete-mode                 ^X^M
delete-global-mode          M-^M
delete-next-character       ^D
delete-next-word            M-D
delete-other-windows        ^X1
delete-previous-character^H
                            ^?
delete-previous-word        M-^H
== MicroEMACS 3.9e (VIEW) == Binding list ===============================
We had been up all night, my friends and I, under the Oriental lamps
with their pierced copper domes starred like our seals — for from them
too burst the trapped lighting of an electric heart.  We had tramped out
at length on the luxurious carpets from the East our inherited wealth,
disputing disputing beyond the extremes of logic and blackening much
paper with frenzied writing.
```

`* MicroEMACS 3.9e ()    futurism    File: futurism`

Figure 42. The apropos command output

Searching and Replacing

It is possible to search in a number of different ways using **emacs**. The simplest type of search, search for a string, can be done as a forward search **^s** or a reverse search **^r**. You may find that typing **^s** causes your terminal screen to freeze up. This is because the **^s** key is being used for data flow control. The terminal can be unjammed using **^q**. **^s** and **^q** are the ASCII XOFF and XON control characters. It is possible that you may wish to rebind this command to another key sequence, or simply always go to the end of the document and reverse search. There is also a search called incremental search, this means that **emacs** starts searching for the first match and gradually refines the matching as each character is typed in. So with our text **swann** if I typed in the incremental search command **^x s** followed first by the character **t** it would move to the word **time**. If I then typed in **h** it would move to the word **that**. If I then typed **o** it would move to the word **thought**. To do a reverse incremental search use **^x r**.

Emacs also has a replace command. The simple find and replace command is **esc r**. This will prompt for each string in the minibuffer, and each string should be terminated by an **esc** character. If you wished to search for an **esc** you would have to use the quote next entry

215

command **^q** this allows the next keystroke to be taken literally and not acted upon. This may suffer from the same problems as forward search and need rebinding. There is a query replace command, **esc ^r**, this prompts for its input in the minibuffer and the input is terminated by and **esc**. When it finds a match it then gives a series of options; to replace, to skip to the next pattern to abort and so on. As with most **emacs** commands, abort is **^g**.

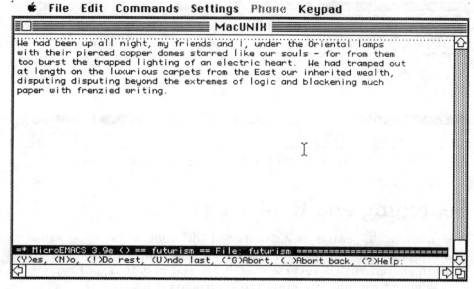

Figure 43. An example of replace query

Keyboard macros

You will often find that you need to do a set of complex commands repeatedly. **Emacs** has a mechanism, called keyboard macros, which allows command sequences to be recorded and recalled. The screen below has a common problem that **emacs** macros can help solve. It is a file of assembly language code that has been imported and the tabs and spaces have gone out of line. What we need to do to rectify this is a sequence of commands. Starting just above the line we wish to reformat we type: **^n** to go to the next line, **^a** to get to the beginning of the line, we can then drop a mark with **esc space**, then use **esc f** to go to the first character in the line. Next we will use delete to mark, **^w**, to delete all the starting white space, then **tab** to format the line.

```
===================== MacUNIX =====================
          ttl            set timer code
 * set up stack, duart, timer and entry point for c programs
        vsect
 stack_top        ds.b    stck            ;stack for c and assembler
 stb              ds.l    1
        endsect

 _init:

                  move.w  #$2600,sr       ;no ints please ipl6
                  move.l  #$c0400,a6              ;set variable data area pointer
                  move.l  #$80800,a7             ;set up stack pointer
        bsr       setup
        move.w  #10000,d0
 delay
        subq.w  #1,d0
        bne       delay
        bsr       main           ;go do the c
 exit:
                  trap    #11
                  dc.w    0,0                    ;back to extended kaybug
        rts                                      ;never get here!
== MicroEMACS 3.9e (WRAP) == setup1.a == File: setup1.a ===================
 [Start macro]
```

Figure 44

We will need to do this several times. If before typing the sequence we
typed **^x(** this will start recording the macro. When we have finished
we tell **emacs** by typing **^x)**. The messages keyboard [Start macro]
and keyboard [End macro] will appear for each command respectively. Now we have recorded the macro it can be recalled by using **^xe**.
If another macro is recorded then the previous one will be lost. There
is a facility to store numbered macros, up to 40, by using **esc x store-
macro** command – this will prompt for a number for the macro. This
requires the use of the recall numbered macro command **esc x exe-
cute-macro-n** where **n** is a number between 0 and 39.

modes

Emacs, like most editors, can be used for a variety of different tasks;
from rudimentary word processing, to program development. Each of
these different tasks will require **emacs** to work in different and probably incompatible ways. For example when coding some C we will
want the editor to automatically indent the next lines of text after the

217

character {. For this to happen during the editing of a letter would be irritating. These different styles of operation are called modes.

It is possible to change **emacs'** behaviour by changing the mode in which it operates. The command **^xm** prompts for a new mode. This can be one of the following:

ASAVE
CMODE
CRYPT
EXACT
MAGIC
OVER
WRAP
VIEW

ASAVE is the auto save mode, **emacs** will automatically make backup copies of its buffers on a periodic basis. The CMODE is fairly straight forward – it's for C programs and it does things like bracket checking. CRYPT allows data to be encrypted on writing and deciphered on reading. EXACT and MAGIC both refer to how **emacs** responds to search patterns; exact is obvious, magic allows regular expressions characters and wild-cards to match. OVER deals with how data is entered; does it overwrite or insert? WRAP is what happens when the text reaches the end of the line, as controlled by fill-column; does it wrap around or continue? Finally VIEW mode allows files to be read but not altered – for example the help screen automatically comes up in view mode.

If you wish to cancel a mode use the **^x^m** delete mode command. Modes can be either local to a particular buffer or they can be global. A local mode is started with **^xm** followed by the mode name or by **emacs** automatically turning on that mode for a particular class of files – files ending in .c for example. Global modes, which will effect all buffers, are turned on by **esc m** followed by the mode name.

Miscellaneous commands

There are a variety of other commands, most of which deal with text display that are useful and deserve mention. The foremost of these is the transpose character **^t** command. This command takes the current character and the preceding one and swops them. For someone with my typing ksills this is a god sedn! There are also a number of commands for changing the case of characters or regions. The **esc u** and **esc l** commands will, respectively, change to upper case and lower case the current word. The command **esc c** will change the current character to upper case. To change the case of a region first you must mark the region then issue the **^x^u** or **^x^l** commands to change the case to upper or lower.

If you wish to repeat an action more than once then **^u** followed by a number will repeat whatever command follows that number of times. So typing **^u22^xe** will recall the current keyboard macro 22 times. **^u** will default to 4 actions. An alternative way of repeating commands is to type **esc** followed by the number of times you wish the command to be repeated.

Sometimes with commands such as **goto-line** you will need to know the line number this can be reported with **^x=** which will report the current cursor position.

    File Edit Commands Settings Phone Keypad

≡≡≡≡≡≡≡≡≡≡≡≡≡≡≡≡≡≡ **MacUNIX** ≡≡≡≡≡≡≡≡≡≡≡≡≡≡≡≡≡≡

```
We had been up all night, my friends and I, under the Oriental lamps
with their pierced copper domes starred like our souls - for from them
too burst the trapped lighting of an electric heart.  We had tramped out
at length on the luxurious carpets from the East our inherited sloth,
disputing disputing beyond the extremes of logic and blackening much
paper with frenzied writing.
```

```
== MicroEMACS 3.9e (WRAP) == futurism == File: futurism =====================
Line 6/7 Col 0/28 Char 352/381 (92%) char = 0x70
```

Figure 45. Status information gained by ^x=

Gaining access to the operating system

When you are using **emacs** it is likely that you will want to gain some form of access to the underlying operating system or some commands. What is described in the following is operating system and implementation dependent, but should run on most implementations of UNIX.

The simplest thing you will wish to do is simply run a command, get its output and then return to your **emacs** task. The key sequence **^x!**, shell command, will prompt, with a **!** in the minibuffer, for the command name. The command will then be executed and its output displayed. **Emacs** will then wait for a key press with the prompt **[END]**, before returning back to normal operation.

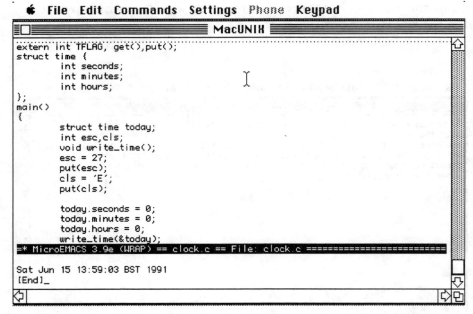

Figure 46. The date command output from ^x!

It is possible that you would want to run a command and save its output into a buffer, using pipe command **^x@** will do this. It will prompt with an @ in the minibuffer and then write the output to a buffer called 'command'. So if we were debugging a C program we could run **lint** on it and use the output in the 'command' buffer to help us.

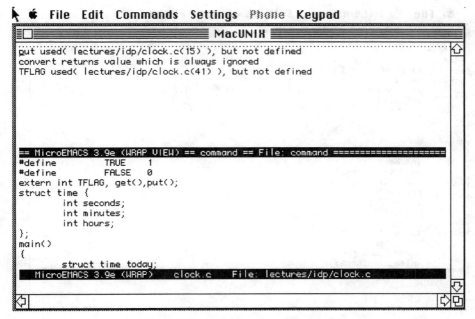

Figure 47. Pipe command output

It also possible to run the contents of a buffer through a UNIX filter and then dump the output back into that buffer using the **^x#** filter buffer command. This prompts for the command with a **#** in the minibuffer and then modifies the current buffer, the buffer that the cursor is currently in. So if we wished to tidy up our C program using the **cb** C beautifier we would type **^x#cb**

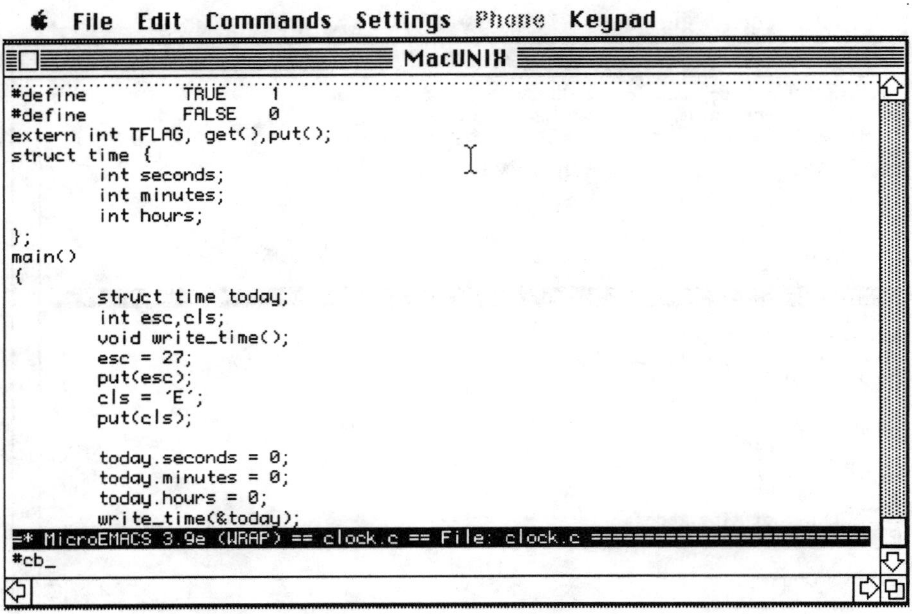

File Edit Commands Settings Phone Keypad
MacUNIX
#define TRUE 1
#define FALSE 0
extern int TFLAG, get(),put();
struct time {
int seconds;
int minutes;
int hours;
};
main()
{
struct time today;
int esc,cls;
void write_time();
esc = 27;
put(esc);
cls = 'E';
put(cls);
today.seconds = 0;
today.minutes = 0;
today.hours = 0;
write_time(&today);
=* MicroEMACS 3.9e (WRAP) == clock.c == File: clock.c ========================
#cb_

Figure 48. Filter command prompt

Sometimes we may wish to do more extensive tasks but not want to leave **emacs.** The commands **^xc** and **^xd** will do this in two different ways. The former runs a sub-shell under **emacs,** which acts like a normal shell except that it is terminated by the **exit** command, and upon termination will return back to **emacs.** The later command will place **emacs** into the background, onto the list of suspended jobs, from which it can be reinvoked by the **fg** command.

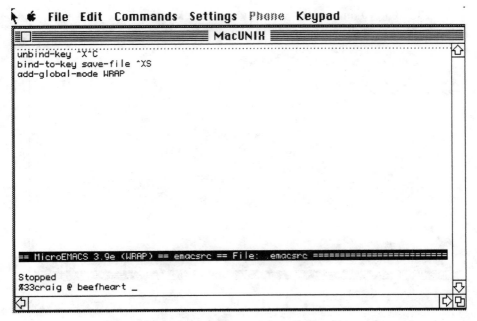

Figure 49. ^xd putting emacs into the background

Start-up options

It is likely that you will want or need to customize **emacs** for your particular needs or site. For example if your computer or terminal server uses the keys **^s** and **^q** for **Xon** and **Xoff** flow control then you will wish to rebind commands like **quote character** and **save file**.

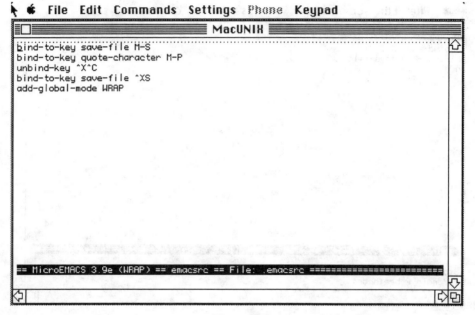

Figure 50

The best place to put such changes is into the **.emacsrc** start-up file. This file of emacs commands is executed each time **emacs** is started up. So to rebind keys you would use the sequence of

bind-to-key command name key sequence

The key sequences are given with **^** for control and **M** (Meta) for escape. Command can be disassociated from keys by the **unbind-key** command. In **.emacsrc** it is possible to make new default modes, run certain commands and so on.

It is possible to find out the full list of key bindings by issuing the unbound **esc x describe-bindings** command. This will list in a buffer named 'bindings list' all of the current key bindings, this will normally be a large number of entries!

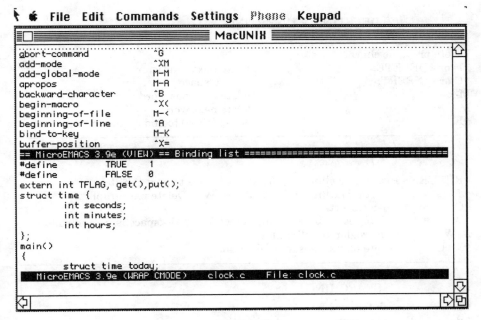

Figure 51

=> ## MicroEMACS 3.8 Help screens

(01/18/87)

M- means to use the <ESC> key prior to using another key
^A means to use the control key at the same time as the A key

^V or [Pg Dn]	Scroll down	M-< or <HOME>	Begining of file
^Z or [Pg Up]	Scroll up	M-> or <END>	End of file

=>   (1) MOVING THE CURSOR

^F	Forward character	M-F Forward word	Keypad arrows
^B	Backward character	M-B Backward word	are active!
^A	Front of line	M-G Goto a line	
^E	End of line	^N Next line	
M-N	Front of paragraph	^P Previous line	
M-P	End of paragraph		

=>   (2) DELETING & INSERTING

<--
Delete previous character

^D or <DELETE>	Delete next character
^C or <INSERT>	Insert a space
M-<--	Delete previous word
M-D	Delete next word
^K	Close (delete) to end of line

=>   (2a) MORE DELETING & INSERTING

<RETURN> Insert a newline	<TAB> Advance to next tab stop
^J	Insert a newline and indent M-^W Delete paragraph
^O	Open (insert) line
^W	Delete region between mark (set using M-<spacebar>) and cursor
M-W	Copy region to kill buffer
^X ^O	Delete blank lines around cursor

=>   (3) SEARCHING

^S	Search forward from cursor position.
^R	Reverse search from cursor position.
^X S	Forward incremental search
^X R	Reverse incremental search
<ALT> S	Search for the next occurence of the last string (IBM-PC only)
<ALT> R	Search for the last occurence of the last string (IBM-PC only)

=>   (4) REPLACING

M-R	Replace all instances of first typed-in string with second typed-in string. End each string with ESC.
M-^R	Replace with query. Answer with:
	^G cancel
	. exit to entry point
	! replace the rest Y replace & continue
	? Get a list of options N no replacement & continue

=>   (5) CAPITALIZING & TRANSPOSING

M-U   UPPERCASE word
M-C   Capitalize word   ^T Transpose characters
M-L   lowercase word
^X ^L lowercase region
^X ^U uppercase region
^Q   Quote next entry, so that control codes may be entered into text

---

=>   (6) REGIONS & THE KILL BUFFER

M-<spacebar> set MARK at current position
^X ^X   eXchange mark and cursor

A REGION will then be continuously-defined as the area between the mark and
the current cursor position. The KILL BUFFER is the text which has been most
recently saved or deleted.

=>   (7) COPYING AND MOVING

^W   Delete (Wipe) region   M-W copy region to KILL buffer
^Y   Yankback save buffer at cursor
Generally, the procedure for copying or moving text is:
  1) Mark a REGION using M-<spacebar> at beginning and cursor at end.
  2) Delete it (with ^W) or copy it (with M-W) into the KILL buffer.
  3) Move the cursor to the desired location and yank it back (with ^Y).

=>   (8) MODES OF OPERATION

^X M   Add mode in buffer   M-M   Add global mode
^X ^M   Delete mode in buffer
          M-^M   Delete global mode
OVER   Replaces (overwrites) rather than inserts characters
WRAP   Turns on word wrap (automatic carriage return).
VIEW   Allows viewing file without insertion and deletion.
CMODE   Automatic indenting for C program entry
EXACT/MAGIC Changes how search and replace commands work
               (see next page)

=>   (9) SEARCH AND REPLACE MODES

EXACT   Uppper/lower case is not ignored in searches
MAGIC   Regular pattern matching characters are active
 .   Matches any one character
 *   Matches any any number of the preceding character
 ^   Beginning of line   [ ] Character class enclosure
 $ End of line   \ Quote next character

---

(10) ON-SCREEN FORMATTING

^X F	Set fill column
Mn-\<tab\>	Set tab spacing to n charecters between tabs stops
M-Q	Format paragraph so that text lies between margins
^X =	Position report -- displays line number, char count, file size and character under cursor
M-^C	Count words/lines/chars in marked region

=> (11) MULTIPLE WINDOWS

Many WINDOWS may be active at once on the screen. All windows may show different parts of the same buffer, or each may display a different one.

^X 2	Split the current window in two	^X O	Change to next window
^X 0	delete current window	^X P	Change to previous window
^X 1	delete all other windows	M-^V	Page down next window
M-^Z	Page up other window		

=> (12) CONTROLLING WINDOWS AND THE SCREEN

^X ^	Enlarge current window	M-\<n\> ^X W	Resize window to \<n\> lines
^X ^Z	Shrink current window	M-\<n\> M-S	Change screen to \<n\> lines
^X ^N	Move window down	M-\<n\> M-T	Change screen to \<n\> columns
^X ^P	Move window up	M-^L	Reposition window
^L	Refresh the screen		

=> (13) MULTIPLE BUFFERS

A BUFFER is a named area containing a document being edited. Many buffers may be activated at once.

^X B	Switch to another buffer. \<CR\> = use just-previous buffer
^X X	Switch to next buffer in buffer list
M-^N	Change name of current buffer
^X K	Delete a non-displayed buffer.
^X ^B	Display buffer directory in a window

=> (14) READING FROM DISK

^X ^F	Find file; read into a new buffer created from filename. (This is the usual way to begin editing a new file.)
^X ^R	Read file into current buffer, erasing its previous contents. No new buffer will be created.
^X ^I	Insert file into current buffer at cursor's location.
^X ^V	Find a file to make current in VIEW mode

=> (15) SAVING TO DISK

^X ^S   Save current buffer to disk
^X ^W   Write current buffer to disk
^X N   Change file name of current buffer
M-Z   Write out all changed buffers and exit MicroEMACS

=> (16) ACCESSING THE OPERATING SYSTEM

^X !   Send one command to the operating system and return
^X @   Pipe DOS command results to buffer
^X #   Filter buffer through DOS filter program
^X C   Start a new command processor under MicroEMACS
^X D   Suspend MicroEMACS into the background (UNIX BSD4.2 only)
^X ^C   Exit MicroEMACS

=> (17) KEY BINDINGS AND COMMANDS

M-K   Bind a key to a command   M-A Describe a class of commands
M-^K   Unbind a key from a command
^X ?   Describe command bound to a key
M-X   Execute a named (and possibly unbound) command {Describe-bindings}
        Display a list of all commands and key bindings to a buffer

---

=> (18) COMMAND EXECUTION

Commands can be specified as command lines in the form:
<optional repeat count> {command-name} <optional arguments>
{Execute-command-line}   execute a typed in command line
{Execute-buffer}   executes commands lines in a buffer
{Execute-file}   executes command lines from a file
{clear-message-line}   clears the message line during execution
 M-~   clears the change flag for a buffer

=> (19) MACRO EXECUTION

^X (Start recording keyboard macro
^X)   Stop recording keyboard macro
^X E Execute keyboard macro
M-<n> {store-macro}   Start recording named macro
    !endm   Stop recording named macro
{execute-macro-n}   Execute macro n (where n is from 1 to 20)

=> (20) SPECIAL KEYS

^G   Cancel current command and return to top level of processing.
^U or   Universal repeat. May be followed by an integer (default = 4)
M-<digit> and repeats the next command that many times.
M-X   Execute a named (and possibly unbound) command

Index

GENERAL COMPUTING BOOKS

Compiler Physiology for Beginners, M Farmer, 279pp, ISBN 0-86238-064-2
Concise Dictionary of Computing and Information Technology, D Lynch, 380 pages, ISBN 0-86238-268-8
File Structure and Design, M Cunningham, 211pp, ISBN 0-86238-065-0
Information Technology Dictionary of Acronyms and Abbreviations, D Lynch, 270pp, ISBN 0-86238-153-3
Project Skills Handbook, S Rogerson, 143pp, ISBN 0-86238-146-0

PROGRAMMING LANGUAGES

An Intro to LISP, P Smith, 130pp, ISBN 0-86238-187-8
An Intro to OCCAM 2 Programming: 2nd Ed, Bowler, *et al,* 109pp, ISBN 0-86238-227-0
BASIC Applications Programming, Parker, 312pp, ISBN 0-86238-263-7
BASICALLY MODULA-2, Walmsley/Williams, 228pp, ISBN 0-86238-270-X
C Simply, M Parr, 168pp, ISBN 0-86238-262-9
Cobol for Mainframe and Micro: 2nd Ed, D Watson, 177pp, ISBN 0-86238-211-4
Comparative Languages: 2nd Ed, J R Malone, 125pp, ISBN 0-86238-123-1
Fortran 77 for Non-Scientists, P Adman, 109pp, ISBN 0-86238-074-X
Fortran 77 Solutions to Non-Scientific Problems, P Adman, 150pp, ISBN 0-86238-087-1
Fortran Lectures at Oxford, F Pettit, 135pp, ISBN 0-86238-122-3
LISP: From Foundations to Applications, G Doukidis *et al,* 228pp, ISBN 0-86238-191-6
Programming for Change in Pascal, D Robson, 272pp, ISBN 0-86238-250-5
Prolog versus You, A Johansson, *et al,* 308pp, ISBN 0-86238-174-6
Simula Begin, G M Birtwistle, *et al,* 391pp, ISBN 0-86238-009-X
Structured Programming with COBOL & JSP: Vol 1, J B Thompson, 372pp, ISBN 0-86238-154-1, **Vol 2,** 354pp, ISBN 0-86238-245-9
The Intensive C Course: 2nd Edition, M Farmer, 186pp, ISBN 0-86238-190-8
The Intensive Pascal Course: 2nd Edition, M Farmer, 125pp, ISBN 0-86238-219-X

ASSEMBLY LANGUAGE PROGRAMMING

Coding the 68000, N Hellawell, 214pp, ISBN 0-86238-180-0
Computer Organisation and Assembly Language Programming, L Ohlsson & P Stenstrom, 128pp, ISBN 0-86238-129-0
What is machine code and what can you do with it? N Hellawell, 104pp, ISBN 0-86238-132-0

PROGRAMMING TECHNIQUES

An Introduction to Z, Imperato, 208pp, ISBN 0-86238-289-0
Discrete-events simulations models in PASCAL/MT+ on a microcomputer, L P Jennergren, 135pp, ISBN 0-86238-053-7
Information and Coding, J A Llewellyn, 152pp, ISBN 0-86238-099-5
JSP - A Practical Method of Program Design, L Ingevaldsson, 204pp, ISBN 0-86238-107-X
Modular Software Design, M Stannett, 136pp, ISBN 0-86238-266-1
Simulation Modelling, Paul/Balmer, 154pp, ISBN 0-86238-280-7
Software Engineering Fundamentals, Ingevaldsson, 248pp, ISBN 0-86238-103-7

Programming for Beginners: the structured way, D Bell & P Scott, 178pp,
ISBN 0-86238-130-4
Software Engineering for Students, M Coleman & S Pratt, 195pp,
ISBN 0-86238-115-0
Software Taming with Dimensional Design, M Coleman & S Pratt, 164pp,
ISBN 0-86238-142-8

MATHEMATICS AND COMPUTING
Fourier Transforms in Action, F Pettit, 133pp, ISBN 0-86238-088-X
Generalised Coordinates, L G Chambers, 90pp, ISBN 0-86238-079-0
Hyperbolic Problems Vols 1&2, Engquist/Gustafson, ISBN 0-86238-285-8
Linear Programming: A Computational Approach: 2nd Ed, K K Lau, 150pp,
ISBN 0-86238-182-7
Numerical Methods of Linear Algebra, S Laflin, 170pp, ISBN 0-86238-151-7
Statistics and Operations Research, I P Schagen, 300pp, ISBN 0-86238-077-4
Teaching of Modern Engineering Mathematics, L Rade (ed), 225pp,
ISBN 0-86238-173-8
Teaching of Statistics in the Computer Age, L Rade (ed), 248pp, ISBN 0-86238-090-1
The Essentials of Numerical Computation, M Bartholomew-Biggs, 241pp,
ISBN 0-86238-029-4

DATABASES AND MODELLING
Computer Systems Modelling & Development, D Cornwell, 291pp,
ISBN 0-86238-220-3
An Introduction to Data Structures, B Boffey, D Yates, 250pp, ISBN 0-86238-076-6
Database Analysis and Design: 2nd Ed, H Robinson, 378pp, ISBN 0-86238-018-9
Databases and Database Systems: 2nd Ed, E Oxborrow, 256pp, ISBN 0-86238-091-X
Data Bases and Data Models, B Sundgren, 134pp, ISBN 0-86238-031-6
Text Retrieval and Document Databases, J Ashford & P Willett, 125pp,
ISBN 0-86238-204-1
Information Modelling, J Bubenko (ed), 687pp, ISBN 0-86238-006-5

UNIX
An Intro to the Unix Operating System: 2 Ed, C Duffy, 152pp, ISBN 0-86238-271-8
Operating Systems through Unix, G Emery, 96pp, ISBN 0-86238-086-3

SYSTEMS ANALYSIS & SYSTEMS DESIGN
Systems Analysis and Development: 3rd Ed, P Layzell & P Loucopoulos, 284pp,
ISBN 0-86238-215-7
SSADM Techniques: Version 4, Lejk, et al, 350pp, ISBN 0-86238-224-6
Computer Systems: Where Hardware meets Software, C Machin, 200pp,
ISBN 0-86238-075-8
Microcomputer Systems: hardware and software, J Tierney, 168pp,
ISBN 0-86238-218-1
**Distributed Applications and Online Dialogues: a design method for application
systems,** A Rasmussen, 271pp, ISBN 0-86238-105-3